SAXMAN

By
Mark Archer
and
Tony Clark

First Edition 2014

Published by
Blowout Sax, South Lodge, North Parade, Bath BA2 4EU.
Tel: 01225 339007. Web: www.blowoutsax.com.
email: markarcher@blowoutsax.com.

© **Blowout Sax 2014.**

Jack Pennington cartoons © penningtondesign.co.uk.
Other cartoons by Paul Rosevear p.rosevear@yahoo.com.
Design and production by penningtondesign.co.uk.

Every effort has been made to locate the artists however if you are any of those unacknowledged please contact Blowout Sax at www.blowoutsax.com.

© Blowout Sax 2014
Mark Archer and Tony Clark

All rights reserved

No part of this publication may be reproduced, stored in a retrieval system, or transmitted in any form or by any means, without the prior permission in writing of the publisher, nor be otherwise circulated in any form of binding or cover other than that in which it is published and without a similar condition including this condition being imposed on the subsequent purchaser.

All paper used in the printing of this book has been made from wood grown in managed, sustainable forests.

ISBN: 978-1-78003-816-2

Published in the UK

Author Essentials
4 The Courtyard
Falmer, East Sussex BN1 9PQ
www.authoressentials.com

A catalogue record of this book is available from the British Library

'Most wretched men are cradled into poverty by wrong; They learn in suffering what they might teach in song.' Shelley, 'Julian and Maddalo.'

There are many excellent books devoted to jazz musicians: histories, biographies, criticism, and we freely admit and acknowledge our debt to them in the creation of our own offering. Mark Archer, as a saxophone teacher, soon realised that most of his students, of all ages, had little or no knowledge of the great saxophonists who had gone before them. It would have been possible to present each of them with a list of books and albums to seek out and devour, but that itself presented a daunting task both for himself as its originator and for his students who would have been easily overawed by both its magnitude and its cost. Furthermore pursuit of such a course suggested a formal approach which was at odds with Mark's teaching philosophy which is unorthodox, effective but, above all else, stresses the fun element. A book was needed that would give some idea of the lives that these men lived, that would convey what was special about their individual style of playing, what their contemporaries thought of them - and what qualities and influence they brought to the saxophone. And since most of the readers would be relative newcomers to the world of saxophonists, it needed to be accessible, informal and, yeah, fun.

After floating the idea to Tony Clark, DJ and lifelong enthusiast, the possibility of the book took shape. Along with his formidable record collection and years of clubbing and concert going, he'd acquired, almost by accident a considerable knowledge of the music and the musicians he loved. This proved useful when he presented his own jazz programme on a Bristol independent radio station for 4 and a half years. At the same time, the aim was to escape from the conventional imagery of existing books on the subject, and introduce a more exciting form of illustration.

So this is the approach we have taken with the Sax Madmen. Starting with Adolphe Sax himself, whose own life and misadventures perhaps unconsciously would set a precedent for many of those who took up and played the wonderful instrument he invented, we chose 14 of the most interesting characters who, in varying degrees, influenced the development of the art of the saxophone. While it would be libellous to label them 'mad' in the medical sense, their dedication to their music, the sacrifices made, and in many cases, the cost to their health, social and family lives, represented a 'beautiful madness' of sorts.

We hope that this book will fill a gap and entertain newcomers and devotees alike. If it provides an insight into the character and music of the artists, and stimulates a desire to seek out more, then so much the better. At the end of the book we list all our sources of information, books which will provide far more detail than we have sought to convey. In addition, we have listed recommended albums that we hope will help you discover and share the wonderful music that the 'Sax Madmen' created.

'Music might tame and civilise wild beasts, but 'tis evident it never could tame and civilise musicians.' - John Gay.

So, The Sax Madmen covered:

1. COLEMAN HAWKINS.
2. LESTER YOUNG.
3. BEN WEBSTER.
4. CHARLIE PARKER.
5. JOHN COLTRANE.
6. ORNETTE COLEMAN.
7. ART PEPPER.
8. STAN GETZ.
9. DEXTER GORDON.
10. SONNY ROLLINS.
11. LOUIS JORDAN.
12. BIG JAY MCNEELY.
13. KING CURTIS.
14. JUNIOR WALKER.

ADOLPHE SAX
1814-1894

"Great spirits have always encountered violent opposition from mediocre minds." - Albert Einstein.

"Everybody loves an eccentric, and when he is also a genius in his chosen field, an obsessional fanatic, extravagent in his loves and hates, hot tempered, impetuous and generally larger than life, who can resist him?" - Paul Harvey.

Your first trip into the wonderful world of sax has to begin with Adolphe, so we present you with:

The Misadventures of Adolphe Sax's Life - 1814-1894.

This is our comic adaptation of the rollercoaster life of Adolphe Sax. This tale deserves to be more widely known as the original Sax Madman, Father Adolphe, was the creator of the golden beast, the dream machine. This man faced endless battles as he strived to forge his imaginary vision into a bright reality. Unlike his namesake Adolphe did not try to conquer the world, but secured his place in history by creating his own... the wonderous world that is The Saxophone.

You will see that Belgium's most famous son was a highly-charged character, as brilliant and eccentric an inventor as he was an arrogant and bumptious individual. Like many touched by genius, he was flawed by being hostile to criticism and lacked any commercial awareness. Now you are aware of these key characteristics let the bumpy ride begin.

Adolphe was born in 1814 in Dinant, the son of a talented instrument maker. At the age of 28 he developed a superior bass clarinet to the current top model and shortly after demonstrating this in Paris, he moved there to live and work. His instruments were acclaimed by musicians and composers alike.

The established instrument makers saw the huge amount of money to be made from Sax and came awooing. Adolphe was

suspicious of their greed and, rejecting their advances, set up his own small factory instead. Hell has no fury to compare with that of disappointed suitors. From the moment that Sax rejected them, the group known as 'The United Association Of Instrument Makers' (with a registered office at the so appropriately named Rue De Serpente) spread an 'aura of malice' over 'this foreign upstart', that was to taunt and haunt Adolphe like ceaseless crucifixion for the rest of his natural life.

The 'Serpentes' set to break Sax as a competitor. When break-ins, burglaries, sabotage, industrial espionage failed to put a stop to Sax's 'upstart' activities, they resorted to mafia-style violence. They tried to roast him in his bed by planting a bomb;

this failed because the explosive device was faulty! They employed assassins to ambush and murder him. However, Sax's habitual arrogance and innate courage sent his would-be attackers on their way. Shortly after this episode a young employee who physically resembled Father Adolphe was brutally stabbed to death as he called at Sax's house - a tragic victim of mistaken identity.

Having failed to destroy him physically, the 'Serpentes' went on the offensive with a set of truly despicable schemes designed to break his spirit. They bribed his book-keeper to keep them informed about the state of Sax's cash-flow, so that they could organise his creditors to demand payment when he was financially weakest. To compound such problems he was naively duped out of a princely 4,000 Francs by a conman.

With Sax on the edge of financial ruin, fate (which certainly owed him some good fortune) finally took a better turn. The influential General De Rumigny was an admirer of Sax's instruments and, on hearing of his precarious situation, prevailed upon the royal patronage of Queen Marie Amelie to bail poor Adolphe out of his financial distress. Not for the last time was our hero saved by friends in high places.

Despite all this unrelenting persecution, Adolphe continued to create and modify instruments, giving birth to the prototype saxophone in 1842.

On the day of the saxophone's public arrival the barrage of

criticism came thick and fast. 'The saxophones sound hollow and wrong - they are noisy and blaring.'

Nevertheless, composers and musicians were becoming increasingly appreciative of Adolphe Sax for supplying superior instruments. In order to demonstrate this beyond all reasonable doubt, his loyal pal Berlioz re-arranged one of his choral works for Sax's instruments, incorporating the saxophone as its centrepiece.

On the day of its premiere performance, Adolphe's saxophone was barely in a fit playing state and was still held together with string and sealing wax. When the moment came for his solo, Sax blew his own creation superbly and, as a finale, he held a sustained note which completely enraptured the audience. The truth was he was grappling with his spare hand to mend the fault on his instrument. A disaster only averted by our hero's quick mind and big, pink, bellowing lungs.

Despite many triumphs and much support for his instruments, Sax was still denied his share of the marketplace by the 'Serpentes' and the orchestras which they bribed to boycott his products. However, there was one part of the market that was beyond corruption - the French military, whose bands collectively represented the largest single purchaser of instruments in France. Aided by the General de Rumigny (top man) once more, Adolphe put his case for a military band based on his family of instruments rather than the traditional format. To decide on the merits of Sax's plan a 'Battle of Bands' was

staged on April 22, 1845 at the Champ De Mars, later to be the site for the Eiffel Tower, witnessed by a festive crowd of over 20,000.

Despite seven of his team being 'nobbled' by the usual conspirators, Sax (with two instruments strapped to his body to make up the numbers) vanquished the competition. This would be the first 'cutting' contest and Adolphe was the victor.

The crowd most enthusiastically acclaimed his success, but the real reward came when The Ministry Of War approved a reformation of military bands to incorporate Adolphe's invention. With no-one to block the use of his instruments, it seemed as if Adolphe had a licence to print money. Shortly after he received notification that his long awaited patent for the saxophone was about to be granted. He was within grasp of a fortune…

But alas, the members of the 'Serpentes' began a continual stream of court cases opposing Sax's patent, and despite his winning of each case it drained Adolphe's resources. This ran throughout his life and, by the end, he had paid out a colossal sum of 200,000 Francs in litigation.

In addition, the 1848 Revolution left Sax defenseless without his royal patronage. At a stroke of a pen the military bands reforms of 1845 were revoked, eliminating the mainstay of Sax's business. Anarchy reigned in Paris. Sax's factory was at a standstill. He narrowly escaped death yet again, as soldiers fired indiscriminately into a crowd where Adolphe just happened to be standing! Yet he still managed to win a Gold Medal at the Paris Exhibition in 1849, and in the same year he was awarded the prestigious 'Legion d'Honneur' for past services.

With Sax's rollercoaster life now at full speed in 1851, another uprising installed Louis-Napoleon as Emperor of France. Once again Adolphe narrowly escaped death. He was in a house from which it was alleged shots had been fired. Sax was condemned to be executed as a rebel sympathiser. However, at the last moment, a music loving General recognised Sax, and hurried him away under his protection.

He survived this danger only to tumble into more calamity. To keep the factory going Adolphe had accepted 30,000 Francs from a benefactor. In 1852, as a result of a hotly contested will, he was confronted by the executors. Foolishly, he admitted it was a loan rather than a gift and, unable to pay back the money, Sax declared himself bankrupt. He was down but not out. There was an amazing comeback when Emperor

Napoleon III, recalling Adolphe's sterling service both to the military and to the world of music, ordered the creditors to absolve him of his debt. Our Champ was back!

And back he came with some right madcap ideas. He designed trombones with 13 bells. He seriously proposed the idea of an orchestra-organ to sound from the hills around Paris so the whole city could hear it. Adolphe's friends howled with laughter until they realized his intensity, and then concerned

for his mental state they advised him to abandon such outlandish schemes, lest he be committed to an asylum. Fortunately he heeded the counsel.

In 1860, still withstanding the constant spectre of conspiracy and harassment, some relief was given when his patents were extended by five years, and that, coupled with the royal patronage, did him little harm. Sax hit his personal moment of glory and recognition at the 1867 Paris exhibition, where he displayed a gold-plated alto saxophone, receiving the highest award of 'Grand Prix'.

Of course, when Adolphe had a high a low was not far behind. He evolved even more hare-brained schemes. The most outlandish of which was the 'Saxocannon'. This prodigious weapon of war was designed to propel a superman size ball weighing 550 tons!

In 1870, he was dealt a crushing blow when his longtime patron and protector Emperor Napoleon was removed in the aftermath of the Franco-Prussian war. Sax also discovered that his formal discharge from bankruptcy in 1852 had not been officially registered, which led to the humiliating removal of his proud badge of the Legion d'Honneur.

With our hero weak and helpless and his patents long since expired, the vultures pounced on his unprotected invention, and, displaying the business acumen which Adolphe lacked, they grew fat. In 1873 he was bankrupt again. In order to clear

his debts, he sold his factory, stock and all his specialised tools. Even his collection of priceless instruments went under the hammer.

His remaining years were spent in near poverty, alleviated partly when he was given a small pension in 1887, as a token recognition of what he had given the world of instrument making.

"I am sorry that I cannot even have a few hours peace in a life eaten by worry."

A bitter Adolphe Sax died in his eightieth year and his lawsuits that had been running for over 50 years stopped. Sax gained fame, but not a fortune.

Even some forty years after his death, his wonderful invention still suffered abuse:

'Posterity will never forgive you Adolphe Sax!' ran the London Daily News headline in 1926. 'The saxophone is a long metal instrument bent at both ends.It is alleged to be musical... The creature has a series of tiny taps stuck on it, apparently touched at random. These taps are very sensitive: when touched they cause the instrument to utter miserable sounds suggesting untold agony. Sometimes it bursts into tears. At either end there is a hole. People, sometimes for no reason at all, blow down the small end which then shrieks and moans as if attacked by a million imps of torture. The shrieks issue from the large end. So do the moans.'

The sax has the ability to upset the sort of people who deserve to be upset. The Nazis viewed the Sax as a symbol of American decadence devised by the international Jewish conspiracy to undermine German youth. 'It seduces them with the degraded music of inferior races played on barbarous instruments.' Their famous Nazi propaganda poster warned of 'entartete musik' (degenerate music) featuring a figure, half-monkey, half-black man (standing for racial impurity) dressed in a top hat (for capitalism) and a star of David (for Jew) blowing a stylised saxophone (for decadence). Also, under Stalin's regime, the Soviets rejected jazz on the grounds of bourgeois-imperialist propaganda and the Saxmen in all state bands were ordered to hand in their instruments.

Fortunately for the rest of the world those seriously evil regimes who dared to disrespect our sax have been destroyed and are regarded with the contempt and hatred they so truly deserved. Meanwhile, the sax has flourished with a vengeance. It now ranks with the guitar and piano as a main solo instrument in all types of music. Its beauty and power have been explored and exploited by some of the greatest musicians the world has ever seen and heard. Many of these more than inherited a trace of the great inventor's wayward approach to life but that truly is another memorable set of tales retold in Sax Madmen.

Adolphe, if only you could see what has become of your creation and how it has brought so much joy to the many millions who listen and the over 20 million who play.

'The Big Blowout' features in the Guinness Book of World Records for the largest saxophone ensemble of all time. Adolphe would have approved!

Photo by Simon Archer.

COLEMAN HAWKINS

**1901-1969
Tenor Sax**

'The only thing nobody can steal from you is your sound... sound alone is important.'

Aka: 'Hawk' or 'Bean' because he knew everything about music.

'HAWK' THE FIRST REAL STAR OF THE TENOR

History acknowledges Coleman Hawkins as the first great improviser on the tenor sax. He was the first to develop a style specially for the saxophone, breaking away from the convention of adapting clarinet techniques. His comprehensive study of musical theory at an early age, a huge tone, undiluted emotion and devotion to the melody, all contributed to 'The Hawkins sound'.

Hawk had his first horn at the age of 9 and was playing professionally at school dances by the time he was 12. After spending his early years playing in small groups and freelancing he was spotted at the ripe old age of 19 by Fletcher Henderson - one of the greatest band leaders of the time. During what proved to be a seven year stay he benefited from the experience of recording and performing with the pre-eminent band of its day and became recognised universally as the Sax Man.

Hawk attributed the secret of his success to 'tune and tone'. By the late 1920s he was established as the Godfather of the saxophone and the greatest influence of his generation. He set the standard for all other saxophonists, and the 'Hawkins school' had more followers in the ranks of musicians worldwide. Everybody aspired to recreate the master's velvety tone on the ballads, and emulate his driving rhythm and swinging phrases on up-tempo numbers.

Even in the 40s and 50s, when his influence was rivalled by

Lester Young and the emergence of the new school of 'Be-Bop' influenced musicians, his musical ability and knowledge enabled him to adapt and remain in the forefront for five decades.

THE HIGHS AND LOWS OF THE HAWK

A short stocky figure, Coleman Hawkins sought to present himself as something of an extrovert. He was a notorious ladies' man, a sociable drinker and smoker, and a stylish dresser, but beneath this facade, he was ultimately a loner.

As a young man his misplaced bravado and arrogance was to teach him an important lesson. Hawk foolishly challenged the legendary Sidney Bechet to a late night 'cutting session'. By dawn, the vastly more experienced and worldly-wise Bechet had 'burned' off his youthful opponent totally. As the chastened Hawk fled down the street, the old master chose to compound his humiliation by keeping step with his prey and blowing even more inspired ideas into his ear.

This deflating experience was to haunt him for the rest of his days, but at the same time created a resolve that it would never be repeated. Hawkins was determined that he would become the master of the cutting contest. He was a great listener, possessing a remarkable talent for memorizing the musical styles of every musician he encountered, and mentally storing their strengths and weaknesses. As he would say, 'Once I play with you, I've got you.'

Over the years, he reigned as the undisputed king of the cutting contests. Like Mike Tyson at his peak, his mere presence intimidated challengers before a note was blown.

It was in this invincible form, that the maestro visited Kansas City in 1934. Prohibition over, the city was bubbling with an incredible range of clubs and bars, an essential stopover for all touring bands. After hours, the clubs were alive with informal jam sessions that often stretched through to the following morning. When Hawkins came to town, both homeboys, Lester Young and Ben Webster, were already in residence. When The Mighty Hawk dropped into 'The Cherry Blossom' club for some small hours blowing, he was unaware of the musical ambush that awaited him. Both the young pretenders had been honing their skills in countless late night sessions, but Hawk, accustomed to his supremacy, was oblivious to their burgeoning talent. As the jam evolved into a cutting session, the Hawk was, for once, under-prepared, and found himself up against the ropes. Webster savoured the battle, but it was Young, in supremely serious shape, who dominated the contest.

Night became morning and exhausted rhythm sections came and went as the combatants locked horns. The great pianist Mary Lou Williams was called from her bed at 4am by an excited Ben Webster and was pressed into adding her accompanying skills to the titanic battle.

Stripped to his singlet, Hawk could not better the future 'Pres' and as midday approached, he stepped from the ring and

walked away from the historic session. He was now running late for a gig in St. Louis, and apparently trashed the engine of his spanking new Cadillac in trying to get there on time. Hawkins the former undisputed Heavyweight Champ of the tenor sax had a serious new rival for his crown.

But occasional setbacks such as these, never diminished Hawkins' stature in the eyes of his fellow musicians. He would always be 'the first', the pioneer, the one who led the way, the original Saxophone Giant. One reason for his longevity at the top was his flexible musical intelligence. Unlike many of his contemporaries he was always ready to explore new avenues. A fine example is the band he led in 1944 which included trumpeter Dizzy Gillespie and drummer Max Roach, front-runners of the new generation and with whom he made what many claim to be the first Be-Bop recordings.

In the sixties Ben Webster, a renowned drinker, was in London and found himself in the early hours with all supplies cut off. Knowing that The Hawk was also in town, he took a cab to his hotel and gained admission to his room. Sure enough Hawk was still up, with his customary bottle of Remy Martin. Despite his desperation for a drink, Webster could not bring himself to ask, and during a spell of agonising small talk, Hawkins neglected to offer. Eventually an exasperated Webster took his leave, mission unaccomplished. He was incapable of asking outright for a drink, 'because it was Hawk.'

However, even the ladies' man Hawkins met his femme fatale. When he was aged 60, Hawk became totally infatuated by a 20 year old goddess of love. This impossible liaison was doomed to failure and left him a lonely embittered man, increasing his brandy consumption to several bottles a day. At the same time, he virtually starved himself to death, eating only one Chinese meal a week. His degradation was complete, when at his last few gigs, he appeared physically and mentally a shell of his former self. The long haired corpse-like figure, shuffling on stage, bore little resemblance to the sharp-suited undisputed Sax King of yesteryear.

HAWK'S 'MOONGLOW'

'Moonglow' is from the album 'The Hawk Relaxes' (OJCCD 709-2). Supported by some talented 'newcomers', as they were in 1961 - including Kenny Burrell on guitar and Ron Carter on double bass - Hawkins is in supreme form through-

out the album which Downbeat accorded four and a half stars, prompting critic John S. Wilson to comment: 'Here (Hawkins) works all his subtle magic, the warm-blooded singing of his playing gliding and soaring through one brilliant chorus after another.'

'Moonglow', one of seven sublime tracks, finds the Hawk in top form. After a striking unaccompanied introduction, he states the melody in typically warm tones, before releasing a series of beautifully constructed variations on the theme. Pianist Ronell Bright and Kenny Burrell contribute fine solos before the man returns for another minute or so of magisterial blowing - relaxed but totally in control!

Fellow legend Miles Davis recalled:
'Bean... you could still hear the melody when he improvised. Amongst the masters, he was the master.'

Hawk On CD
1. The Essential Keynote Collection. Mercury 830960/2.
2. The Hawk Flies High. Original Jazz Classics. OJ CCD 027.
3. Coleman Hawkins and Roy Eldridge 'Live At The Opera House.' Verve 521641/2.
4. Coleman Hawkins encounters Ben Webster. Verve 823120/2.

Here's a list of some of Hawk's recordings for you to check out: *Close Your Eyes, Laura, I love Paris, Like Someone In Love, Cross Town, Picasso.*

LESTER YOUNG
1909-1959
Tenor Sax

'I like playing cool...'

Originally known as 'Red', he will be remembered forever as 'Pres', the title bestowed by the immortal Billie Holiday: 'When it came to a name for Lester, I always felt he was the greatest, so his name had to be the greatest. The greatest man in the country around then was Franklin D. Roosevelt and he was the President. So I started calling him The President.'

THE PRESIDENT'S STYLE

Young's style was unique, and a departure from the guidelines set by Coleman Hawkins who was the supreme influence at the time. Whereas the Hawk's tone was big, heavy and full of vibrato, by contrast Young's was light and feathery, yet at the same time both soft and supple.

Nimble and fleet on fast numbers, and tender on the slow, this introverted lyricist had a dry, almost vibrato-less sound, which was to become the role model for the 'cool' school of playing. It was this playing style and tone that came under criticism even from fellow Count Basie band members. Tenorist Herschel Evans, a Hawkins disciple asked him: 'Man, why don't you play alto? You've got an alto tone.' Pointing to his head Young replied: 'There's some things going on up there. I think some of you guys are all belly.'

On the other hand Dexter Gordon, the saxman 14 years his junior, was more appreciative, reflecting in later years: 'Pres had an entirely new sound, one that we had been waiting for, and he was the first one to really tell a story on the horn.'

This was because Pres was always absorbed by the melody of the songs and played with gentle restraint.

THE PRESIDENT'S LIFE

Young was a law unto himself, and cut a most unconventional figure. He became a mythical lonely character with his ever-present pork pie hat, long black coat down to his ankles, hair hanging down onto his shoulders (20 years before Hippies). Even the way he held his 'axe' at a 45 degree angle went against convention. Young also invented his own jargon, a language understood by himself alone. The expression 'cool' was his description of his style. Pres would also call colleagues and club-owners 'Lady' with a straight face and total conviction. He would call white people 'gray' and a black person an 'Oxford gray'. And as for his ancient Pan-American horn it was held together by rubber bands, glue and chewing gum, and when his keys were bent, Pres moaned: 'My people won't play!'

Other Young-isms were 'I feel a draft...' meaning racialism was in the air. This was never more apparent than in the Deep South when he and Budd Johnson missed the tour bus after a bender. When the white train conductor refused them entry, Johnson flashed a pistol and as they strode past the white passengers ('ofays') Young clapped his hands with delight, exclaiming: 'Shoot your pistol, baby! Shoot your pistol.'

Lester Young had a long and famous musical love affair with the sublime Billie Holiday. Although strictly platonic, on stage they achieved a lyrical and harmonious liaison that would be the envy of any married couple. It was the Pres who returned the compliment of bestowing nicknames. During a long inter gig journey that they shared in Count Basie's band bus, the other musicians sought to relieve the boredom by exchanging reminiscences of previous sexual triumphs, true or imagined. As they became increasingly lurid, a more sensitive member of the band called a halt by reminding them 'Hey fellas, there's a lady aboard' - to which the previously silent Young added 'Yeah, Lady Day!'

His approach to life was often bizarre, he terminated his long residency with the Count Basie band, by failing to turn up for a recording session on Dec 13th 1940. The guy sent to wake him reported back to Basie: 'Pres says go away and let him sleep. Man has got no business making music on Friday the 13th.'

At the Newport Jazz festival trumpeter Ruby Braff saw Lester Young sitting alone in the afternoon sun near the stage, and quite oblivious to his situation, he was smoking a joint in public. The following conversation ensued: 'Pres, what are you doing?'
'Where are we?'
'What do you mean where are we! We're at the Newport Jazz Festival!'
Lester half-closed his eyes and took another toke: 'Then, let's be festive.'

As another of our sax giants Sonny Rollins observed: 'Lester Young was very cool and by himself in a world all of his own.'

Sadly, Young's world was shattered in 1944 by his brief but brutal spell in the army. Suddenly deprived of any musical experience and subjected to a discipline totally alien to his maverick lifestyle, he was caught smoking dope, his only available solace. Inevitably he was court-martialled and spent time in a hostile Georgia military prison before returning to civilisation in 1945. With hate storming into his serene life, this crushed much of his sensitivity, lyricism and tenderness. Meanwhile, during his enforced absence from the scene it seemed other hornmen were imitating Lester Young better than he could.

Burnt and disillusioned, he indulged in more and more booze. In the 50s, Young became a pale reflection of his previous greatness and he returned home from a spell in Paris to die quietly, at the 'musician's graveyard' - The Hotel Alvin. The President was only 49.

THE PRESIDENT'S 'STARDUST'

This Hoagy Carmichael classic provides a perfect vehicle for Pres' consummate skill with the ballad.

Like all the best saxmen, he had great respect for the lyrics, believing that an understanding of the words was an essential pre-requisite to interpreting the music. No doubt inspired by the numerous hours accompanying Billie Holiday, he employs a vocalists' phrasing as if he is blowing the words through his horn.

As critic Dave Gelly has stated: 'His playing remained the window on his soul.' His performance of 'Stardust' is a textbook example of this approach.

Trumpeter Ruby Braff, a spliff abstainer, and a musician never noted for his generosity with compliments, was moved to comment: 'He was so in love with the melody, every 4 bars he paints a beautiful picture. And he never, never does anything less than that. Even in his sickest period when he was half

dead and his mouth couldn't even get onto the mouthpiece properly, he played with better form than anyone who's healthy. He was the master composer.'

Pres on CD
1. The Complete Aladdin Recordings. Blue Note CDP 832787/2.
2. Billie Holiday and Lester Young. Fremaux FA013.
3. The Lester Young Trio. Verve 521650/2.
4. Jazzmasters 30. Verve 521859/2.

Here's a list of some of Lester's recordings for you to check out: *I Can't Get Started, D B Blues, Undercover Girl Blues, All Of Me, I Didn't Know What Time Was, Lester Leaps In.*

BEN WEBSTER
1909-1973
Tenor Sax

Aka: 'Frog', from his bulging eyes.

'I'm gonna blow this goddamn horn until they lie it down on top of me...'

Paintings by David 'Shan' Shanahan.

THE DEFINITIVE STYLE

Alongside Coleman Hawkins and Lester Young, Ben Webster completed the Tenor Triumvirate - the three great pioneers who achieved so much in establishing their instrument as one of the most potent solo voices in the jazz orchestra. Although he was influenced by Hawkins, fourteen years his senior and the Godfather of Sax, he developed an individual and totally unmistakable style of his own. His forte was the ballad for which he created a sensuous, breathy romantic tone, almost erotic in its intensity.

It was the perfect vehicle for expressing deeply felt emotions - 'middle of the night recollections of other nights not spent alone.' He had the ability to seemingly float each musical phrase and leave it quivering on puffs of air. This was his musical signature.

However, on uptempo numbers Webster employed a coarser tone coupled with aggressive muscular phrasing. While with Duke Ellington, in 1940, his solo on 'Cotton Tail' endeared him to dancers and to an emerging school of tenor players alike. His raw, primitive blowing would subsequently provide inspiration for a whole generation of honkers and screamers to come. To the listener it provides an almost shocking contrast to the refined lyricism of his ballad style. Sure, ballads would predominate as his career progressed, but it was reassuring to know that when the blues or down home numbers demanded it, he could always call on the earthier side of his musical armoury to produce a harder edge to his sound. When the chips were down he could be a musical brawler with the best of them. It was confirmation that, as in real life, Mr. Webster was not all sweetness and light.

THE LIFE OF BIG BEN

A fellow Kansas City boy, Ben Webster benefited from being taught music by Lester Young's father and gaining his first experience of the club scene by accompanying his teacher's son on piano. Taught the rudiments of the sax by another friend, Budd Johnson, throughout the 30s he served his apprenticeship with the bands of Benny Moten, Cab Calloway and Fletcher Henderson. But it wasn't until he joined Duke Ellington in 1940 that his talent as a supreme soloist was to flower. The Duke, ever astute, recognized his saxman's potential and created numerous solo opportunities for him. Playing alongside the extravagantly gifted altoist Johnny Hodges did him no harm and from under the wing of the Ellington orchestra he flourished and grew to become one of the great influential voices on the tenor.

From an early age he had an appetite for alcohol, good food and exciting company. When off duty he appreciated the nightlife and all the temptations it had to offer, but he was also a proud man who liked to project his image.

When he was with Cab Calloway's band, after the gig whatever city he was in, Webster was always ready to go out jammin' in the clubs. Calloway's bass player Milt Hinton recalls: 'He'd change into something real sharp, grab his horn and go to a little club and sit in. Always, he made the grand entrance - in a dark club, he'd instantly light up a cigarette on entering, illuminating face like a spotlight. Heads turned, people would see the horn case and knowing Calloway was in town, the buzz would go around the club 'Ben Webster's here'.'

Webster was also known as 'The Brute' due to his strength and occasional demeanour. Once he attempted to demonstrate this quality while clubbing with his friend, World Heavyweight Boxing Champion Joe Louis. When challenged to give his best shot to the solar plexus, Webster staggered the Champ, with the power of his blow. Unfortunately, Webster's misplaced bravado led him to urge the 'Brown Bomber' to reciprocate, with the result our saxman spent the rest of the evening receiving attention for his cracked ribs at the local hospital.

Perhaps due to his early exposure to the ways of Lester Young, Webster also developed his own hip vocabulary. This personal rap was particularly effective in intimidating the local 'square' musicians. They must have been totally bemused when confronted with: 'Put the frame on that lane. It's a possible calf and cow.'
This of course meant: 'Look at the suit that guy's wearing - must've cost 150 dollars.'

As a solo artist he toured extensively and made frequent visits to Europe, where his appearances were ecstatically received and financially well rewarded.

In the 60s he was a welcome visitor to Ronnie Scott's club in London, but travelling seemed to exacerbate his already considerable alcohol consumption! On one occasion the club owner had to collect him from Victoria station where, having fallen from his carriage, he became jammed in the gap

between train and platform. Once extricated, the 'relaxed saxophonist' was conveyed on a luggage trolley to an awaiting cab. Webster was a chronic alcoholic and in later years more often than not was intoxicated when he performed on stage. After a session at Ronnie Scott's a customer complained Webster talked more than he played. Scott's retort was: 'I'd rather hear Ben Webster talk than 90 percent of tenors play.'

His final years were spent in Copenhagen which became his base from which he gigged around Europe. Sadly in his latter years, his drinking habit far exceeded his musical output and he died in 1973, during a playing engagement in Amsterdam. That night he practically predicted his own death and expressed his own epitaph: 'You're young and growing... and I'm old and going.'

WEBSTER'S 'TIME AFTER TIME'

Webster's ability, to interpret a ballad is unchallenged. There are literally hundreds of recorded items, in a wide range of settings, but perhaps the greatest example of Webster's magic, is from 'Ben Webster & Associates', (Verve 835254-2) 'Time After Time'.

After a gentle piano intro, Webster enters in all his seductive glory. The breathiest tenor in the business takes over and instantly goose-pimples and hairs on the back of the neck testify to the wondrous sound that he creates on this track. Effortlessly, he states the slightly melancholy theme and then proceeds to wring intense passion out of each chorus, with each perfectly selected cluster of notes. The impact on the listener is devastating - Webster seems, through the warmth of his horn, to have total control over our inner feelings and thoughts. It is an act of complete emotional manipulation, a moment in time when the horn player's artistry reached a peak which has never been surpassed.

While serving in Bath's specialist CD shop, a wonderful testimony to Webster's lyrical powers was overhead. A smart lady of 'a certain age' required in a refined voice 'some jazz saxophone, nothing raucous - you know, ballads and standards.'

On hearing Webster's breathy sensual tones coming through the speakers with shattering effect, the well-spoken lady gasped: 'Oh my god, I almost had an orgasm.' Needless to say she became an instant Webster devotee, but we did warn her, marvellous as he was, the album did not come with a guarantee!

Fellow tenor saxophonist Johnny Griffin remarked: 'Ben's sound was so warm and enveloping and he could play one note and you could play 100 notes, and he could get more effect out of one note than you'd get out of 100.'

The avant-garde saxman Archie Shepp, whose later more mellow sound was compared to Webster. 'I feel more and more humble everyday about that because I think he was one of the most sophisticated and perfect voices on the instrument that I've ever heard.'

Years previously when working in a New York dive, the most expensive lady in the establishment paid Webster a priceless compliment. Dismissing a would be client's persistent demands, she exclaimed: 'Get this straight, I never do business when Ben's playing.'

Ben Webster On CD
1. Ben Webster & Associates. Verve 835254/2.
2. See You At The Fair. Impulse GRP 11212.
3. Soul of Ben Webster. Verve 527475/2.
4. Soulville. Verve 833551/2.

Here's a list of some of Ben's recordings for you to check out: *Chelsea Bridge, Where Are You, In The Wee Small Hours, In A Mellow Tone, Willow Weep For Me.*

CHARLIE PARKER
1920-1955
Alto Sax

'Life used to be so cruel to musicians, just the way it is today. They say that when Beethoven was on his deathbed, he shook his fist at the world because they didn't understand. Nobody in his own time ever really dug what he wrote. But that's music.'

Nicknames: 'Yardbird', 'Bird' because on tour the car Charlie Parker was in, hit a chicken on the road. He ordered the driver to stop and he went back for the 'yardbird'. When he arrived at Lincoln he asked the landlady of the boarding house to cook it.

Painting by Michael Pell.

PARKER'S 'BE-BOP'

His alto sax tone was arguably the most expressive voice in jazz, with the feel of the blues, from the depths of a soul in torture. Bird was a visionary, one of the original creators of the new music 'Be-Bop'. It was like music compressed, each sparkling phrase sounding endlessly manic.

While Bird was more renowned for his magnificent playing, his equally creative partner trumpeter Dizzy Gillespie, was responsible for the music's sartorial identity. Sporting a goatee, beret and glasses he made Be-Bop fashionable by adding an image of glamour and sharpness.

Their cascade of melodies and dialogue together were a revolution and proclamation of the new direction.

'Bird' and 'Diz' would think and play fast, deliberately starting and ending their phrases in really odd places, just to confuse and bewilder anyone who had the audacity to try to 'sit in'. They also toyed with the volume (dynamics), varying the range of tone from a gentle whisper to loud outcry. While adding to the unexpected thrilling danger of Be-Bop, at the time it rendered the music unhummable and therefore, nigh on impossible for the masses to comprehend.

While Bird had paid homage to the Godfather Hawkins' strength and Young's light tone and lyricism, he forged his own unique sound.

There was the usual opposition to change. When Ben Webster walked into Minton's and witnessed Bird for the first time, he said: 'What the hell is that up there? Man is that cat crazy?' And he walked up to Bird and snatched the sax out of his hands saying: 'That horn ain't s'posed to sound that fast.'

Miles Davis recalled: *'Bird changed the minute he put the horn to his mouth... he went from looking like a real down and out to having all the beauty just bursting out of him... amazing transformation... he could play like a motherfu**er even when he was falling down drunk and nodding off behind heroin... Bird was something else... He was notorious in the way he played musical combinations of notes and musical phrases.'*

THE BRIEF LIFE OF A 'HIGH-FLYING BIRD'

The film 'BIRD' (directed by Clint Eastwood) offered a thin portrait of Charlie Parker. This filmic biography lacked Parker's hell-raising energy which gave birth to Be-Bop and turned it into an underground religion. By concentrating on the decadent aspects of his character, it gave an unbalanced image of the man and failed to credit his amazing creativity and the inspiration he gave to others during and after his life.

Miles Davis called him 'a greedy motherfu**er... most geniuses are. He wanted everything... he pawned his sax, his suit to get heroin... he dressed in baggy clothes that looked as though he'd slept in them for days... face all puffed up... eyes swollen and red... but he was cool with that hipness... confidence...

everyone treated him like a king...'

He once showed his arm to a friend saying: 'This is my Cadillac,' and holding out the other arm, 'and this is my house.'

Miles Davis: *'Bird himself was almost a God... attracting all kinds of women, dope-fiends... people giving him gifts... so he took and took, missing gigs and sets.'*

On one occasion, mentally cracked he started a fire in a friend's apartment and ran screaming naked through the hall before attempting suicide.

Leonard Feather: *'Charlie drank more and more in a desperate attempt to stay away from narcotics while still avoiding the terrors of a sober reality.'*

On the onset of his final illness the Doctor asked Bird: 'Do you drink?' He winked and said in a mock English accent: 'Sometimes I have a sherry before dinner.'

Eventually years of over-indulgence and physical self-abuse took their toll. He was bloated, constantly exhausted and even his playing became a parody of his true brilliance - that is, if he bothered to show.

When Parker died at the apartment of Princess Pannonica de Koenigswarter, a wealthy jazz patron, the doctor who completed his death certificate assumed he was 55 not 35.

History recognises Bird as one of the greatest innovators who virtually single-handed, changed the direction of jazz irreversibly. Despite his perverse and often anti-social behaviour, his music transcended all and he was loved and respected by musicians and public alike.

Pianist Walter Bishop Jnr. considered his time accompanying Charlie Parker was a 'dream gig'. Bishop's reminiscence of his time with Parker exposes a different facet on Bird's character. While touring with Parker they always had sessions with local musicians sitting in and he fondly recalls a young John Coltrane in Philadelphia, Sam Rivers and Jaki Byard in Boston. However there were musicians of far less talent and technique who would invariably mess up. 'But Bird would always find something they could do and compliment them on it. He was an inspirational force. Bird knew everybody had something.'

Immediately after his death, the slogan 'Bird Lives' appeared as graffiti around New York, but the expression is just as current today. His music and style has influenced every practitioner of the jazz saxophone.

CHARLIE PARKER'S 'SCRAPPLE FROM THE APPLE'

This performance of 'Scrapple From The Apple' (see Dial Masters below) was a staple of Parker's repertoire which was recorded in 1947. Like so many Be-Bop numbers, it was based on standards, in this case a combination of 'Honeysuckle Rose' and the ubiquitous 'I Got Rhythm.'

After the piano introduction, Parker and Davis state the theme in unison, and then Bird cuts loose. It is easy to understand his nickname 'Bird' for, when he solos, it's as if a cage has been opened and he has been set free to soar above the rest of his companions. Playing here at mid-tempo, one is more than able to appreciate his dexterity, ideas, and phrasing. The notes seem to bubble from his horn with a relaxed logic. This serves as an unforgettable snapshot of Bird in full flight.

Dexter Gordon on Bird's playing even 30 years later: *'The fluidity, freedom of expression, musically and emotionally are still unbelievable.'*

Miles Davis: *'He was so original... a soloist... Nobody could play like Bird, then or now... the greatest alto saxophonist that ever lived.'*

Bird on CD

1. Charlie Parker, The Dial Masters. Spotlite SPJ (CD) 109-2.
2. Yardbird Suite, The Ultimate Charlie Parker Collection. Rhino R272260.
3. Jazz At Massey Hall. Original Jazz Classics OJC20044-2.
4. Charlie Parker, Complete Norman Granz Mastertakes. Definitive DRCD 11273.

Here's a list of some of Bird's recordings for you to check out: *Melancholy Baby, Klactveedstene, Parker's Mood, Summertime, Swedish Schnapps, Now's The Time, Loverman.*

JOHN COLTRANE
1926-1967
Tenor and Soprano Sax

Aka: 'Trane.

'You just keep going all the way as deep as you can. You keep trying to get right down to the crux.'

Painting by Ewan David Eason.

COLTRANE STAGES OF CREATION

John Coltrane really became established as a result of his successful and fruitful association with the illustrious Miles Davis and his quintet in 1955. He took temporary leave in 1957, and managed to cleanse himself of drugs and booze forever as part of his spiritual awakening.

In 1958 he rejoined Miles, with the addition of Cannonball Adderley on alto, now leading a sextet, and helped create the magnificent 'Kind Of Blue' album, rightly acclaimed as the greatest jazz album ever. Coltrane's contribution was immense, his powerful playing providing a foil to Miles Davis' sparse trumpet.

Miles Davis: 'Trane loudest, fastest saxophonist I ever heard... he could do it and was phenomenal... it was like he was possessed when he put that horn in his mouth... he was so passionate, fierce yet so quiet and gentle when he wasn't playing.'

Soon after, Coltrane split from Miles and announced his solo career with the astonishing 'Giant Steps' album, the first of a series of classics recorded for the Atlantic label. The modal approach using scales as opposed to chords, had been the basis of the music on the 'Kind Of Blue.'

Ever the musical explorer searching constantly for new areas of self-expression, Coltrane developed this method of writing and playing for his own purposes. The results were described by critic by Ira Gitler as 'sheets of sound' - an expression that remains Coltrane's tag. His phrasing and runs were so fast that it was like a piano player striking chords rapidly, with each being highlighted separately. Critic John Wilson was prompted to state: 'He plays his tenor sax as if he were determined to blow it apart.'

Miles Davis states that from the 1960s onwards John Coltrane was 'by now on a mission... messed up enough (whose) only concern was music and growing as a musician. That's all he thought about... seduced by the beauty of music.'

When he 'doubled' up (playing 2 different types of sax) with the soprano he sought out eastern and middle eastern influences and his unique tone, initially ugly and plain, soon entrances in an hypnotic way. Miles Davis went on to say that 'with the soprano in 1960, (Coltrane's) style changed... played like no-one but himself - lighter, faster - he could hear and think better on the soprano... after a while it sounded like a human voice wailing.'

Gil Evans, producer: *'Coltrane had an original sound... I'd sit and bathe in that sound.'*

Trane was now the innovator, intensely seeking the ultimate freedom of expression. His controversial album 'A Love Supreme' (1964), was a great prayer of hymnic intensity and passion, the music building and becoming ever more powerful. This spiritual creation reached out and influenced all races. He was a beacon in a time of black awareness, expressing feelings with notes, defining his 'philosophy without words.'

Indeed, in San Francisco today there is a church dedicated to John Coltrane, with a huge icon of the man who is seen as the patron saint of 'a soul search for a spiritual community.' Its Bishop Franzo King also says: 'John showed us the harmonising properties of music and the universality of the language of music... John Coltrane's music can move people away from hate and anger and violence towards the realm of praise to God and services to man.'

It is remarkable that when, many years before, Coltrane was asked what he would like to be in 10 years time, he prophetically replied 'a saint.'

It was to Trane that the jazz world turned for the next dynamic development in music. The revolutionary torchbearer rewrote the Saxophone method book again, just like Hawkins, Young and Parker had done before him.

His untimely death just when his work had become very avant-garde and almost definitely not his journey's end, provoked chaos in the free jazz movement because he was its acclaimed leader.

PARABLES OF SAINT JOHN

The man himself was an obsessive, relentlessly studying musical theory and would play in a curious, mesmerizing virtuosic way. Of this need to continually realize his potential Coltrane said: 'We have to keep on cleaning the mirror.'

However, he was always unhappy with his tone and tried hundreds of mouthpieces to obtain a better sound. He was similarly haunted by embarrassment over his crooked teeth, hence there are no photos of him in full grin. This created a false impression that he was a moody, introverted individual.

In his search Coltrane would blow a 20, 30, 40 minute solo as he developed his ideas further and further. Once after playing 27 choruses, when Coltrane said he didn't know how to stop, Miles suggested: 'Try taking the horn out of your mouth.'

Or once in a while Miles might say: 'Why did you play so long, man?' and Coltrane would say: 'It took me that long to get in.'

COLTRANE'S 'MY FAVOURITE THINGS'

From the most unlikely source, 'The Sound Of Music', Coltrane's soprano sax sung a wonderful new interpretation of 'My Favourite Things', especially when he releases from the main melody, building up and accelerating his runs using Arabic and Indian scales.

Having witnessed a live performance of 'My Favourite Things' at Birmingham Town Hall in the early 60s, Tony Clark recalls 'the whole set was astonishing, especially his 20 minute solo, which was never self-indulgent. Chorus after chorus re-interpreted the melody supported by the mesmeric piano of McCoy Tyner. One of the greatest musical experiences of my life.' Miles Davis on this cultural phenomenon: *'Not only was he a great and beautiful musician, but a kind and spiritual person... his creative imagination... a genius, like Bird. But music is what he left us.'*

On 'Kind Of Blue' Coltrane's sound is aural seduction, on 'Love Supreme' it is the agony and the ecstasy, but by the time of his demise, there was precious little ecstasy detectable in his playing, rather a relentless often painful search for perfection.

'Trane on CD
1. Blue Train. Blue Note CDP 746 0952.
2. Giant Steps. Atlantic 781337/2.
3. My Favourite Things. Atlantic 782346/2.
4. A Love Supreme. Impulse 11552.

Here's a list of some of 'Trane's recordings for you to check out: *Naima, After The Rain, I Wish I Knew, Locomotion, Dahomey Dance, Russian Lullabye, Aisha.*

ORNETTE COLEMAN
1930-
Plastic Alto Sax

'To create music that flows like water.'

Painting by Chris Daly.

COLEMAN'S FREE JAZZ

Now this was a hornman who really broke every rule. His revolution was to try and make music as natural as breathing. He delivered this 'free jazz', 'living music' and played off-pitch, discordant and vocalised 'cries' which were loose, upsetting many in the same way as Bird and Pres.

Blowing through a plastic sax to relay the message he found it absorbed the sound less and 'you could almost see the shape of the breath of a note.' The goal of Coleman and fellow rebel, Don Cherry's miniature trumpet was to produce a style of music called 'Harmolodics'. No-one had heard that degree of freedom before. This approach liberated the duo to blow their own story. He viewed his alto sax as having four basic voices, those of a soprano, bass, tenor as well as the alto range.

Coleman, as an 'expressionist', was the first truly free musician. He believed that written music stifled natural expression, so each track had no rigid framework. The freedom was stretched to permit the individual to play in his own tuning. Notes would be bent up and down, off-pitch, experimenting with all the amazing sounds that the sax could make. It became an alliance with the unknown.

His unique creation has been subjected to the full range of musical criticism. Initially 'grotesque, filled with anguish and chaos', then a degree of reluctant tolerance and eventually it progressed to 'beautiful and captivating'.

Ah, the vagaries of the music press!

Miles Davis: *'I liked Ornette as a person... But I didn't hear anything that was revolutionary... just the 'new thing' in town... at the beginning spontaneous playing 'free form' bouncing off what each other before, only they were doing it with no form or structure, and that's the important thing.'*

Ornette established a whole new school of playing, Free Jazz, influencing Trane who would talk and watch Coleman play his 'instant art' with great abandon.

Nowadays, he's still in the forefront of the music scene, sometimes marrying Free Jazz with the funk of Steve Coleman's M-Base group, while still creating new and innovative music of his own.

ORNETTE COLEMAN'S ROUGH RIDE TO FREEDOM

Because of the treatment Coleman received from the music critics and the general public, he felt alone, distrustful of society, paranoid of being 'ripped-off' by promoters and record companies alike. It was hardly surprising that Miles Davis was prompted to say: 'Ornette's a jealous kind of dude. Jealous of other musician's success.'

Another maverick possessing an iron-will, his style prevailed and, as noted, he gained a measure of acceptance, after considerable delay.

A native of Fort Worth Texas, he spent his early days playing R&B in juke joints. Unfortunately, he chose to experiment with weird off-beat scales, and not only was he beaten up by the patrons of the dance but his sax was thrown off a cliff. For years, anyone who heard his playing branded him a 'freak'.

He would be thrown off the bandstand for playing too many strange notes and the rawness of tone was considered offensive to the ears of both patrons and fellow musicians.

A.B. Spellman offered a typical example of his rejection: 'He went to sit in with Dexter Gordon one night, and Dexter had characteristically, not shown up in time for the first set. Ornette went up to play with Dexter's rhythm section only to have Gordon come in and order him off the bandstand. He said: "Immediately, right now. Take the tune out and get off the bandstand." And Ornette made the long walk back to Watts in the rain.'

After another rhythm section just packed up and left during the middle of one of his solos, unruffled Coleman was heard to have said: 'No matter how much you get rejected, you put in that much more study and work into it so you can produce more.'

His life seemed to have been punctuated with a succession of bizarre often painful adventures. He developed a wacky dress sense, perhaps as a further reaction to the sharp-suited forerunners of the sax, such as Webster and Hawkins whose music he'd turned his back on. He would turn up to gigs in psychedelically coloured garments, looking more like a circus clown than a serious musician. At one point, driven to the edge by an accumulation of sexual hangups and frustrations, he tried to persuade his Doctor to castrate him - fortunately without success. He even added his ten year old son to his band as a drummer, convinced that the psyche between father and son would enhance the musical output.

In 1962, he took a sabbatical from public performing in order to learn how to play the trumpet and violin. When he unveiled his new found 'skills' on his return three years later, the resultant sounds were received with no enthusiasm by the critics, and worse still were publicly debunked by both Miles Davis and Charlie Mingus.

Despite the rebuffs, scorn and even humiliation, Ornette's spirit burned fiercely and could not be extinguished. Over the years his originally small following has grown from a cult to full blown recognition. He will never be welcomed into the ranks of 'easy on the ear' performers but to this day he retains the renegade streak, and is now accorded acceptance as the figurehead of the avant-garde.

In the present context his earlier work sounds far more accessible and less outrageous than when it was launched on an unsuspecting public. Like so many great men whose talent and idiosyncrasies we have documented in this book, he has never lost that manic quality that separated him from his contemporaries.

He remains a true innovator and a genuine Sax Madman.

ORNETTE COLEMAN'S 'LONELY WOMAN'

'Lonely Woman' is taken from the 1959 Atlantic album, 'The Shape Of Jazz To Come'. Ornette is accompanied by Don Cherry, cornet, Charlie Haden, bass and Billy Higgins, drums. 'Lonely Woman' was a composition which is just out of tune, falling tantalisingly between beauty, ugliness and weirdness. That was the appeal.

The two horns play the theme before Coleman takes over the solo spot. During a sequence of phrases, he builds up tension, his sound at times is guttural, more often wailing. Cherry punctuates his leader's onslaught with a few terse phrases of his own. But it's Coleman's track and he blows free over the top of the metronomic rhythm until rejoined by Cherry, he arrives at a logical conclusion.

His partner Don Cherry said: *'Style is only related to a certain period - Ornette's goes beyond.'*

Ornette on CD

1. The Shape Of Jazz To Come. Atlantic 781339/2.
2. Free Jazz. Atlantic 781364/2.
3. At The Golden Circle, Stockholm. Blue Note B21Y 84224.
4. Sound Museum. Harmolodic/Verve 531657/2.

Here's a list of some of Ornette's recordings for you to check out: *Blues Connotation, Embraceable You, Morning Song, Harmolodic Be Bop.*

ART PEPPER

1925-1982
Alto Sax

'There are a lot of parallels between a criminal and a jazz musician... If I had a gun on a robbery I would love using it... filled with hate... hate and beauty are so close.'

Painting by Francis Strickland.

THE ART OF PEPPER

Influenced by Bird, Art Pepper had a searing often desperate tone. His phrasing was irresistibly mesmeric and full of emotions, because of a broken unpredictable style of running up and down the sax as opposed to smooth legato runs. But Pepper had the natural ability to play 'hot' or 'cool' with equal dexterity. In later life his playing matured, and exhibited a yearning passion and heartfelt conviction.

When playing he confesses to an out of body experience when he's looking at himself: *'I love that I feel like a God... a trance that is all-powerful.'*

Pepper, believing he was a genius, rarely practised. In 1957, there was a typical demonstration of this ill-disciplined approach. Because of drugs and other distractions, Pepper had not been performing regularly. In collusion with the head of Contemporary Records, Pepper's then wife Diane arranged for him to record with Miles Davis' rhythm section, acknowledged as the finest in the country - Red Garland, piano, Paul Chambers, bass, and Philly Joe Jones, drums.

Diane only informed her strung out husband of this coup on the morning of the session. To compound his anguish, his sax, due to neglect, was in a mess and he had to make do with a taped up mouthpiece. He had not rehearsed with the band and was totally in awe of their reputation. 'They're masters. Practising masters.' The tunes were chosen almost at random, some composed jointly during the session, yet out of this chaotic situation, Pepper played magnificently.

The album 'Art Pepper Meets the Rhythm Section' received rave reviews including a 5 star rating from the doyen of the jazz magazines, 'Downbeat'.

PEPPER'S 'STRAIGHT LIFE!'

After an unhappy childhood, Art Pepper showed all the signs of an original Sax Madman. He embarked on a career of 'stealing, hustling, boozing, fixing, stashing, scoring, robbing ceaselessly searching for my kind of high.' Pepper loved getting a 'hit' from good heroin which he claimed solved his crazed dreams, in which the rejection by his fifteen year old mother who had attempted to abort him, featured heavily.

However, due to his addiction, Pepper spent some of his best years incarcerated in prisons, including a fourteen month spell in the notorious San Quentin where he was totally deprived of any musical experience.

All this is vividly described in his autobiographical book, 'Straight Life'. This brutally honest account totally alienated his only daughter, who branded him a 'rapist and a racist.'

It describes him as a young man, who was a fiendish heartbreaker, possessing handsome roguish looks coupled with a mammoth ego, which he exploited to the full in satisfying his well documented sex drive. However, compare photos from these happier days with those of later years, and the contrast is horrific. The intervening period fuelled by his addiction to drugs, booze, sex and cigarettes took a massive toll on him physically, and virtually destroyed his constitution. His cause was not helped by an incompetent surgeon who mutilated his body during a botched operation on his stomach.

In 1969, after years of drug abuse, Pepper was admitted to Synanon, the famous drug rehabilitation centre, where he resided for two years. He emerged a changed man, in no small part down to the influence of another resident, who became the last love and the greatest influence on the rest of his life, Laurie Miller, the third Mrs. Pepper.

The following anecdote reveals not only how he played but how he lived his life. During a residency at San Francisco's Black Hawk Club, the legendary Alto Sonny Stitt dropped by for a 'cutting contest.' As Pepper expressed it: 'It's a communion. It's a battle. It's an ego trip. It's a testing ground and that's the beautiful part of it.' They agreed to play the acid test of musicianship 'Cherokee' and Stitt, who was really 'flying', proceeded to rattle off some 40 choruses during the course of an hour. 'He did everything you could play, as much as Charlie Parker could have played if he'd been there.'

The gauntlet had been thrown down with a vengeance, and, as usual, Pepper was not in the best of shape for such a challenge.

'I was strung out... hooked... drunk... having a hassle with my wife Diane, who'd threatened to kill herself in our hotel room next door. I had marks on my arm and thought there were narcs in the club, and all of a sudden I realised it was me. I had to put up or shut up or get off or forget it or quit or kill myself or do SOMETHING.'

In such a harrowing circumstances, he started to blow and 'I forgot everything and everything came out. I played way over my head. I played completely differently than he did. I searched and found my own way, and what I said reached the people. I played myself and I knew I was right and the people loved it and felt it. I blew and blew and when I finally finished I was shaking all over: My heart was pounding: I was soaked in sweat and people were screaming.'

This and the recording session with the Miles Davis Rhythm section seem to summarise not only Pepper's musical experience, but his whole way of life. For so much of his time he was battling against the odds, even if most of these monumental problems were of his own creation. And yet, when intimidated or scared by what he was facing, he would throw himself totally at the challenge. This indomitable spirit would sustain him above his self-destructive habits. It was this life force, with a lot of support from Laurie, that enabled him to find real happiness and ease his twisted and bitter feelings. He recognised his debt to her, with 'Our Song' which he confessed had taken him fifty five years to write.

In this Post-Synanon period, Pepper seemed to sense that he was on borrowed time and that every performance could be his last. Consequently, his playing took on an intensity and beauty that is almost painful to behold. His unpredictable nature had almost destroyed him and the faith of his friends and loved ones, yet out of this tortured existence, he created some of the most beautiful, powerful and intensely emotional jazz ever performed on the Saxophone.

PEPPER'S 'HERE'S THAT RAINY DAY'

This track from the album 'Living Legend' is a fine example of the passion and feeling that seemed always present during this later phase. As we know, Pepper had experienced more rainy days than most. There is a deep felt sadness throughout his playing on this track, a painful beauty that conveys some of the despair that he experienced during his turbulent life. Pain

Jack Pennington's cartoon was sketched 'live' in about two minutes whilst watching Pepper play at Ronnie Scott's in 1978.

could never be more bitter-sweet. In Art Pepper's words: 'It's a ballad I really love. I think I enjoy playing ballads more than anything else. You can pour your soul into them, you can say everything.'

Art Pepper ON CD
1. Art Pepper Meets The Rhythm Section. Original Jazz Classics OJCCD 338.
2. Living Legend. Original Jazz Classics OJCCD 408.
3. Thursday Night At The Village Vanguard. Original Jazz Classics OJCCD 694.
4. The Art Of Pepper. Blue Note 746853/2.

Here's a list of some recordings by Art for you to check out: *Our Song, The Trip, Red Car, Arthur's Blues, Ophelia, Nature Boy.*

STAN GETZ
1927-91
Tenor Sax

'The four greatest virtues a Jazzman can possess - taste, courage, individualism and irreverence.'

Nickname: 'The Steamer'. Given by the master pianist Oscar Peterson who came up to Getz and said: 'You ain't from the cool school, you! Ha! You're the Steamer! It's nice to be cool sometimes, but it's also nice to know you can steam.'

THE SUPREME STYLIST

Like many of the Sax Madmen, Getz was a child prodigy. At school, he discovered his amazing ability to sight-read, was blessed with a photographic memory for music scores, and was also the possessor of perfect pitch. At the age of 15, while touring with Jack Teagarden, he was introduced to the excesses of alcohol. And shortly after, as a member of the illustrious Stan Kenton's orchestra, he discovered heroin. These twin addictions were to remain and virtually control the majority of his life.

Stan was a confirmed disciple of Lester Young's 'cool school' of sax - Lester, said Getz, 'was the first tenor saxophone player I heard play melodically.' The air buoyancy of Pres, was overlaid with a more guttural 'Jewish ache' as Getz called it. From these influences, Getz was to create a unique style which was to become the envy of his contemporaries and latter day saxophonists alike, with, as critic Dave Gelly expressed it: 'Phrases that hung in the air like wreaths of smoke.'

He embraced the language of Be-Bop which added breadth to his expression, but he never sacrificed melody, which was forever the foundation of his playing style.

In the early 60s, he experienced a musical change of direction, as significant to his career as Be-Bop had been. When guitarist Charlie Byrd played him some recordings he'd made in Brazil, Getz was at once beguiled by the languid rhythm and subtle melody of the Bossa Nova, which he realized offered rich possibilities as a setting for his floating, ethereal melodic tone.

He and Byrd recorded the 'Jazz Samba' album, which astonishingly topped the pop music charts and established Getz as a household name. First America then the world was seduced by the infectious rhythm of the bossa nova. Getz was at the forefront, collaborating with the emerging stars of this Brazilian phenomenon Antonio Carlos Jobim, Luiz Bonfa, Astrud and Joao Gilberto amongst others. The music achieved astonishing record sales and featured heavily in the pop charts. Suddenly jazzman Stan Getz was elevated to the status of rock star, with earnings and public recognition to match.

STAN GETZ, BEAUTY AND THE BEAST

Stan Getz was a frightening contradiction - capable of playing the most lyrical, sensitive jazz saxophone ever heard, and yet susceptible to the most depraved drunken rages, during which nothing and nobody was safe. His musical output could best be described as 'beauty from the beast'.

His first wife, Beverly, was a singer and, like him, a teenage heroin addict. As a successful member of the Woody Herman band Getz managed to support their burgeoning drug dependency. There he was one of the famous 'Four Brothers' with fellow tenors Zoot Sims, Jimmy Giuffre and Al Cohn, all Lester Young disciples, and all heroin addicts. On Baritone, was the virtuoso Serge Chaloff, who doubled as their supplier. At one gig, the band was on the same bill as a circus. During the show a gigantic performing bear almost lost control and lashed out over the heads of the sax section. The only straight member, Altoist Sam Marowitz, ducked, Getz and his companions were too stoned to react. Totally oblivious to the danger all escaped unscathed.

Stan Getz was a renowned ladykiller. Bassist Bill Crow recalled: 'He always had five or six girls. He had them all in different rooms in the same hotel, and one night they were all sitting at the table in front of the bandstand, while he played. And each of them thought she was with him.'

When it came to the crunch though, heroin outweighed his sexual appetite. Proof was an incident when the screen goddess Ava Gardner, newly divorced from Artie Shaw, and hot to trot spotted the young, baby faced Stan Getz and was totally entranced. But he displayed his true colours and priorities by making his excuses and chasing after his dealer who had just entered the room!

In 1953, Getz tried to hold up a drugstore. It was an episode which mixed black farce and tragedy. From gaol Getz wrote to the Downbeat editor. 'I shouldn't have been withdrawing from narcotics while working and travelling. With the aid of barbiturates I thought I could do it. Going into this drugstore, I demanded some narcotics. I said I had a gun (I didn't). The lady behind the counter evidently didn't believe I had a gun so she told another customer. He, in turn, took a look at me and laughed, saying "Lady, he's kidding you. He has no gun". Having flopped at my first 'caper', I left the store and went to my hotel. When I was in my room I decided to call the store and apologize. In doing so my call was traced and my incarceration followed... I'd had enough of me and my antics... it's pure and simple degeneracy of the mind, a lack of morals.' These are the words of a sublime hypocrite.

Another unsavoury aspect of his character emerged when, in a car accident, his son sustained a multiple skull fracture. In the same accident his wife Beverly suffered a broken back and was encased in a full body plaster cast. While she was totally immobilised, Getz chose the moment to announce that he was leaving them for Monica Silverskiold, a beautiful twenty-one year old student from an aristocratic Swedish family!

But Monica was soon made aware of Stan Getz's dependencies, and rapid changes of personality. On their first holiday in Kenya part of his courtship comprised consuming large quantities of drugs and alcohol; and, during the course of the inevitable rage that followed, he broke her nose and cheekbone. Amazingly, on their return to Sweden, she announced their engagement!

Over the years, Monica made repeated efforts to help him find a cure. She sought distinguished medical advice and for his part he made many visits to rehab clinics. All were dismal failures, and only interrupted his consumption. His drunken outbursts persisted and Monica and their children were regularly beaten and terrorised. Eventually he abandoned her for Jane Walsh, a girl half his age who had successfully undergone drug rehabilitation.

After many years of humiliation, Jane finally got him to 'kick' booze and drugs, and for the last five years of his life he was 'clean.' As a reward, Getz drifted out of her life and formed another relationship with Samantha Cesena who was in her early twenties. By then he had contracted cancer of the liver, and after a short-lived success in fighting it, he eventually succumbed to its grip in 1991.

Getz's one concession to a healthy lifestyle was a lifelong love of swimming. In the 60s, while playing in London at Ronnie Scott's, he was enjoying a late night drinking bout with Spike Milligan and Peter Sellers at his hotel, The Dorchester. He bet his two admirers that he could swim the Thames, and to their amazement, he descended from his room, clad in trunks and bathrobe. After taking a taxi to the riverside, he plunged in. Alarmed by the strength of the currents, Milligan phoned the police for assistance. In a drunken voice, he identified himself as one of 'The Goons', which failed totally to convince the duty officer who advised him to go home and sleep it off. In the clutches of panic, he and Sellers leapt into a cab which took them to the other side of the Thames. There, they were greeted by a relaxed Getz, who enquired 'What kept you guys?'

GETZ'S 'THE FOLKS WHO LIVE ON THE HILL'

'Girl from Ipanema' is his most famous song with Astrud Gilberto where the blend of her soft vocals and his soothing fills created a big hit, seducing a worldwide audience. However, 'The Folks Who Live On The Hill' dates from 1960, recorded in Copenhagen which was for many years his adopted home.

He plays a solo throughout the four minutes plus, gently exploring the ballad without any gimmicks or fireworks. Indeed, he seems barely to depart from the melody throughout, but nevertheless the performance is a superb example of 'the beautiful sound.'

He starts at a slow tempo, with a dryish tone, but 'blows the words' smoothly through his horn. The tempo starts to pick up and a subtle swing is detected. Occasionally, Getz blows more forcefully, before returning to the gentler mood of the piece. He implies that he could cut loose at any moment but instead chooses to stay true to the feel of the slightly sentimental song. His sound remains warm and luxuriant throughout, but the suggestion of controlled power removes any threat of cloying sweetness.

'Let's face it, we'd all like to sound like that - if we could.' John Coltrane.

Getz On CD
1. Focus. Verve 821982/2
2. Pure Getz. Concord CCD4188.
3. Getz and JJ Johnson: At The Opera House. Verve 831272.
4. Getz/Gilberto. Verve 810048/2.

Here's a list of some of Stan's other recordings for you to check out: *East Of The Sun, Night Rider, Spring Can Really Hang You Up The Most, Samba Triste, Blood Count.*

DEXTER GORDON

1923-1991
Tenor Sax

Aka: 'Long Tall Dex'

'My concept of sound was that it should be powerful. The heavyweight kind. And the sound comes from what you hear in your mind. Obviously, if that's what you hear, eventually it'll come out. For me the sound develops.'

Painting by Jean Tyrell.

DEXTER GORDON: A CULTURED GIANT

The unlikely star of the cult film 'Around Midnight', a 6ft. 4' colossus, who handled the tenor sax like a toy. His playing of ballads has a spine-chilling quality which lives long in the memory. It was a combination of his beautiful tone and heavy-weight sound that made him a musical figurehead who was to influence Getz, Coltrane and Rollins.

In the 40s and 50s this Herculean giant played with a hard-edged tone ranging from high-register screams right down to the bottom note, a technique honed by frequent cutting contests in the jazz dives of L.A. Dexter and his friendly rival Wardell Gray created the notorious track 'The Chase' which emerged from their tenor duel while originally playing 'High Society.'

'It was nothing less than combat, a duel in which weapon of choice was neither pistol nor dagger, foil or sword - just a tenor saxophone... To a degree it was one of those things, to be the fastest, the hippest. The tenor saxophone player with the biggest tone - that takes balls, that takes strength.' This seven minute track was the biggest selling jazz single on the Dial label, outperforming even Bird's records.

From 1962 to 1977, like many other American jazzmen, Dexter chose to live in exile in Paris and Scandinavia. It was during these years that his tone mellowed as his reputation as a wonderful interpreter of ballads grew. On the 'Ballads' album, his version of 'Misty' is exquisite, turning a classic standard saxophonist's cover into a sensitive individual statement.

In 1977, he returned as a hero to the American jazz public and stayed producing albums that celebrated the roots of this saxophone giant.

There are two trademarks associated with the name Dexter Gordon. After finishing a solo he would hold his sax horizontally in space, his symbolic way of saying 'Thanks' to the audience. Also, he was rightly famous for his laconic but eloquent announcements, a touching example of which follows. At the end of a performance 'I hope we have put some dreams under your pillow tonight.'

LONG TALL DEX: RELUCTANT MOVIE STAR

Bernard Tavernier (the French director of the film 'Round Midnight') said on meeting Dexter: 'Everything in him is musical... He is Be-Bop in walking... he dominates the film with that amazing gravel-toned scarred voice with his own ad-libs like "happiness is a wet Rico reed" plus his visual dominance. He was dying when he made the film from a near lifetime of abuse, drugs and alcohol and a face that looks as if it's been to the limit. Dexter was playing himself and he was the star.'

As Dexter himself put it: 'The film's aim is to show that musicians are dedicated - a lot of good men self-destructed out of frustration.'

Once, when scoring heroin, Dexter played a solo on 11th and 5th Avenue for his pusher. 'He had just gotten me so high, so when he asked me to play, I unpacked my horn and blew right there on the street corner.'

Dexter was composer, musician, and actor in Jack Gelber's play of drug addiction called 'The Connection.' However, on completing a two year stretch for drugs, he maintained that he made the best of these 'enforced vacations' from narcotics to rebuild his abused body.

He explained jazz's high drug related mortality rate thus: 'Look, you were working in dives and bars, harmful stuff was all around and in the air... a little difficult to remain Mr. Clean in such circumstances, you know.'

When performing in a club, a drunk stumbled up to the stand where Dexter was playing and dropped a handful of coins into the bell of the sax - without pausing he opened one eye, shut it and finished the solo. After he tipped the money out, ambled to the bar bought himself a drink, and toasted his benefactor.

Late one evening Dexter was relaxing in his dressing room between sets at the Keystone Club, when an overly exuberant female fan came barging in and tripped over one of his super-sized feet. Unflustered, he nonchalantly caught the falling lady around the waist and carefully sat her down on the sofa next to him. After a pregnant pause, he gently broke the awkward silence by saying: 'My shoes may be dusty, but my soul is clean.'

DEXTER GORDON'S 'HEARTACHES'

This is a track from his Blue Note album, 'Gettin' Around' 1965. Though entitled 'Heartaches' Gordon is in no mood for brooding, and states the melody at a swinging mid tempo. From there on he hits a finger popping groove and his big-toned blowing leaves no room for sadness. His exuberant playing with inventive phrasing, muscular sound and effortless ability to swing are all exhibited to perfection on this number.

Long Tall Dexter Gordon plays like he looks, as Jackie McLean calls it 'fabulous and grand.'

Dex On CD
1. Doin' Alright. Blue Note CDP784077/2.
2. Our Man In Paris. Blue Note CDP 746394/2.
3. Biting the Apple. Steeplechase SCCD 31080.
4. More Than You Know. Steeplechase SCCD 1030.

Here's a list of some recordings by Dex for you to check out: *The Shadow Of Your Smile, The Chase, You've Changed, Love For Sale, 'Round Midnight, I'm A Fool To Want You.*

THEODORE SONNY ROLLINS

**1929-
Tenor Sax**

'I think my whole life has been a work-in-progress... I play to reach myself.'

Aka: 'Newk'. In the 50s he bore a striking resemblance to the then Brooklyn Dodger pitching ace Don Newcombe.

Painting by Cate Archer.

THE RHYTHM KING OF SAX

Sonny Rollins is the rhythm king of the sax, master of blowing the main themes and then weaving away from the tune, subtly changing the melodies but maintaining a constant logic to his improvising. He leaves you with sly echoes of the original theme, avoiding repetition, like a chain-smoker sparking a new phrase from the end of the old one.

Live, one is struck by his muscular and powerful tone and whirlwind movements, as he swings the bell of the horn through the air. 'There are certain parts of the room where the horn just projects better, where the sound is more friendly... I'm trying to find that 'sweet spot'. That's very important... they are those where the horn talks back to you - and you hear what they're hearing.'

It was alleged that the twin challenge of Coltrane and Coleman to his supremacy contributed to his most famous 'disappearance' from the music scene in 1959. In an interview with Ben Sidran he put a different, less sensational slant on his motives. While critics and fans alike lauded his every performance and rated him, numero uno of the tenor, he felt that 'I didn't have the feeling within myself, that I was really able to put out what they expected from me.'

Ever the seeker of perfection, he decided 'to lay off the scene and get these things.' It was during this period of re-assessment that the legendary 'Bridge' stories originated. The truth was some nights he chose to play either solo or with selected friends on the bridges of New York, but his favourite was the Williamsburg Bridge. 'It was beautiful because you were playing against the air... I could play as loud as I wanted to, and just go through anything.' After a couple of years he returned rejuvenated, having undergone another phase of his 'continuous evolution', with his amazing inventiveness and vitality enhanced.

Musically he is capable of blending the styles of calypso, rock and Be-Bop. His characteristic approach was to take a tune, explore its melody and then in the immortal words of pianist Stan Tracey, 'shake the arse out of it' reconstructing it in as many different guises as his fertile imagination can concoct. Every solo becomes a voyage of discovery, keeping the audience on the edge of their seats fascinated by the variations that he fashions from the basic melody. The tension is only released by his final resolution of the musical conundrum he's set himself.

'I don't even want to know I have the horn there - I want the music to play itself.'

THE ECCENTRIC COLOSSUS

In his constant pursuit of musical excellence, he has also gone through a number of chameleon like changes. From a skinhead, to an Arab dressed complete with robes, he has also experimented with a range of headgear including a French beret and a Stetson (check the sleeve from his 'Way Out West' album). Another favourite item of apparel was a belt with a row of tambourines attached.

Apart from his voluntary sabbaticals he also took some enforced absences due, as ever, to a flirtation with substance abuse, inspired by hearing that Billie Holiday and Bird were using drugs. 'The drugs were to shut out everything but the music.' Rollins ended up briefly in prison, living like 'an animal'.

Fortunately, he was able to kick the habit after seeing the legendary pianist Bud Powell, pass out after shooting up some bad shit. The traumatised Sonny thought he'd overdosed. To purge himself of the addiction, he worked fanatically on his physical and mental fitness. He dropped out of the music scene and took manual work in the construction industry until he was totally 'clean'.

He created one of his trademarks on his first visit to Ronnie Scott's Jazz club. As he stepped out of the cab he started playing his tenor and continued while descending the stairs to the astonished delight of the audience.

Once, while wandering about stage at an open air concert in New York, Sonny, keen to get closer to the audience, leapt into the crowd. Unfortunately he misjudged the height, and for a moment disappeared from view. Suddenly his unique sound was heard and our unperturbed hero poured out more inspired phrases, while lying prone on his back. He finished the set, leaving everyone unaware that he'd broken his ankle!

Today, one of the 'Grand Old Men' of the saxophone, he tours only sparingly, but once on stage he is as dynamic as ever, improvising endlessly, pacing the stage in his constant search for the elusive 'sweet spot.' Afterwards, this strikingly dignified Giant is the epitome of humility, speaking individually to the numerous fans who stay behind to meet him, and thanking THEM for their patience!

SONNY'S 'ST. THOMAS'

Sonny is one of the great and rare sax survivor whose playing spans over five decades. With such an accumulated body of work to choose from, how does one select a solitary track to represent a man of such diverse genius?

1956 was a prolific year for Rollins recordings and out of many sessions 'Saxophone Colossus' (Prestige CDJD002) was acknowledged as a masterpiece. So we chose the favourite track from the album. Rollins' ancestry can be traced back to the West Indies and he probably grew up with this tune and others of similar origins.

Max Roach sets the mood with a Caribbean drum introduction and then Rollins blows the calypso inspired melody. The saxman is in exuberant mood as he plays above and below Roach's infectious rhythm. He explores the theme, before laying back for Roach's drum solo. He returns in full force, ideas pouring out in an unending stream. Briefly the piano maintains the happy mood, before Rollins ties it all up neatly by bringing everyone back home to the original theme.

If ever a jazz sax track could be called the sound of summer, by virtue of its effervescent tone and carefree mood, this would be a major qualifier. It's Rollins on top form.

Our regular contributor and critic Miles Davis was impressed: *'Sonny... a legend. He was an aggressive, innovative player who had fresh musical ideas... he's still a great player.'*

Sonny himself said: 'I think my whole life has been a work in progress. I've had a beautiful life, and I've played with some of the most fantastic musicians.'

Sonny On CD

1. Tenor Madness/Saxophone Colossus. Prestige CDJCD 002.
2. A Night At The Village Vanguard Vol 1. Blue Note CDP746517/2.
3. Way Out West. Original Jazz Classics OJC CD 337.
4. Sonny Rollins+3. Milestone MCD 9250/2.

Here's a list of some more Sonny recordings for you to check out: *When Your Lover Has Gone, Old Devil Moon, God Bless The Child, Green Dolphin Street, Alfie's Theme.*

LOUIS JORDAN
1908-1975
Alto Sax

'I loved playing jazz... Loved singing the blues... But I wanted to be an entertainer - that's me - on my own. I wanted to play for the people, for millions... Jazzmen play mostly for themselves... I want to play for the people.'

THE ULTIMATE ENTERTAINER

Louis Jordan was one of the most influential musicians of all time. At first reading this probably sounds rather unlikely. This clowning, joking singer/comedian who also played sax and led a band of entertainers - how could he be a pivotal figure in the development of the music scene?

Well he achieved it on more than one level. As a singer he became one of the first 'crossover' artists. He was encouraged by his songwriter partner Dan Burley to write about black life - food, drink, relationships, hard times, partying, work, domestic incidents, good and bad. Each song was like a black cartoon depicting stories and incidents that a black audience could recognize at once. However, his self-mocking humour, catchy tunes and infectious dance orientated rhythms also caught the imagination of the white public. Unlike most black R&B artists with really heavy regional accents, Louis Jordan's enunciation, his 'golden voice', was clear and distinct, really easy on the ear. He had a never ending stream of national hits - 'Choo Choo Ch Boogie', 'Saturday Night Fish Fry', 'Caldonia' to name a few. Even titles of his songs entered the national consciousness - 'Open The Door Richard', 'Ain't Nobody Here But Us Chickens', 'Is You Is Or Is You Ain't My Baby' became catchphrases adopted by all races in America.

Louis Jordan had set out to become 'the modern Bert Williams' one of the most gifted clowning musicians of his race. Instead he was recognised as the master showman who won over a larger multi-racial audience than any other previous black artist, save for that other Louis, a certain Mister Armstrong. He did much to further the status of the black entertainer at a time when segregation was still widely practised in the States, either brutally in the South or more subtly in the so-called emancipated North. Jordan referred to it as 'straddling the fence', a state he achieved through his dignity and his infectious sense of humour.

He never resorted to 'Uncle Tom-ing' or the exaggerated negro caricatures adopted by many of his contemporary black entertainers in a bid to gain acceptance by the white market. Uncompromisingly, his songs were about black life and, if white folk gained pleasure from them, it was due to their own merits - quality, lyrics and tunes, humour, musicianship and sheer dance-ability.

LOUIS JORDAN, DIRECTOR OF JIVE

The man was joy and festive fun, his whole exuberant personality flowing through his voice, even performing with an outsized pair of white framed glasses (pre-dating Elton John) to radiate humour.

'I decided that when you come to see Louis Jordan, you'd hear things to make you forget what you'd had to do the day before and just have a good time, a great time.'

'With my little band, I did everything they did with a big band to make the blues jump.' His singing, song-writing and supreme showmanship should not disguise the fact that he was a brilliant saxophonist and outstanding band leader. He was never a ground-breaking stylist like the saxophone giants Coleman Hawkins, Charlie Parker, Sonny Rollins and John Coltrane. But, as a small group saxophonist, he was supreme and set the standard for all R&B groups that followed. He achieved it through sheer hard work and dedication.

An incident in his formative years influenced his attitude to rehearsals: He was only 9 years old but already a member of his local Brinkley Brass Band, of which his father James was a senior member. Precociously talented but easily bored, he messed about to impress his less talented peers during a rehearsal. His father who was in charge on that occasion, was so enraged that, for the first and last time, he boxed Louis' ears. Shocked and embarrassed in front of his friends it was a lesson hard learned, but never forgotten. For the rest of his musical career he approached rehearsals with total dedication and sense of purpose. When he led his own bands he applied this same philosophy to all members and if anybody strayed, instead of boxing ears, he exacted fines. That early lesson from his father was to define his lifelong regard to discipline in all he and his bands attempted.

At the age of 15 he was now a member of his father's dance band The Rabbit Foot Minstrels. A fellow member was a 14 year old alto player by the name of Lester Young. Friendly rivalry developed into a cutting contest, with Louis playing soprano sax. Over a series of dance numbers and blues the battle raged, at the end of which the supremely gifted Lester had totally vanquished our hero.

This incident too was to prove cathartic. Previously Louis had total confidence in his ability as a musician, but the encounter with his younger rival had exposed his shortcomings. He realised he had much to learn and henceforth he devoted hours to practise daily and applied himself with the same rigour and dedication as he had to rehearsing. His technical skill and improvisational ability became his strengths and established him as one of the Saxophone Giants of the small groups. He was an inspiration to the likes of Joe Turner and Louis Prima who modelled their bands on the style of his Tympany Five with the saxophone solo a feature of every number. In rock'n'roll years even Bill Haley and his Comets churned out hit after hit using the same musical template.

His talent as a musician and entertainer was acknowledged and acclaimed by some of the most prestigious talents.

Art Pepper fellow sax madmen: *'I heard Louis Jordan on the alto, he knocked me out.'*
Nat King Cole: *'He is one of the great performers. I would give top ratings to anything he does…'*
Ray Charles: *'Louis Jordan had a great and lasting influence upon my appreciation of music and even my performance.'*
Sonny Rollins, the Saxophone Colossus: *'He was like the bridge between the blues and jazz. He had a great big sound on alto and I just loved him.'*
For James Brown, the Godfather Of Soul: *'He was everything'* - and apart from his musical talent, that almost certainly included the strict discipline he enforced on his bands - a philosophy that Mr Brown notoriously took to extremes.

Louis progressed through a number of local Arkansas bands before moving to Philadelphia working with bigger named bands led by Charlie Gaines and violinist Leroy Smith. However, it was his two years with the illustrious Chick Webb that brought him to the forefront. He emerged from the horn section to have a featured cabaret spot recreating the Deacon Jones spoof preaching act from the minstrel shows. He was a natural showman with a flair for comedy - something that was always present even when he led his own band. While with Chick Webb he was a member of one of the most popular bands in the hugely competitive dance scene. He was involved in regular battle of the bands where the two famous swing orchestras competed against each other in front of a ballroom audience. One famous battle at New York's Savoy Ballroom involved Chick Webb and Benny Goodman, the King Of Swing. With an audience of 4,000 and another 5,000 locked out on the street, Chick Webb's orchestra triumphed and continued to do so until he eventually went down to the Duke Ellington Orchestra.

By 1939 a highly skilled musician and a recognised crowd pleaser, Louis formed his own band, The Tympany Five. The band established a huge following in Harlem before breaking through in the rest of the USA. Radio broadcasts, regular hit records and highly successful juke box films raised his profile and he was a household name. During the 1940's he and the Tympany Five were featured in several films - Follow The Boys, Meet Miss Bobby Sox, Look Out Sister - and many more.

Louis Jordan achieved superstardom through his rigorous disciplined approach to practising, rehearsing and performing. Unfortunately offstage this moral fortitude was rarely present - and his personal life was quite chaotic. He was always a gambling man and with the cash rolling in from his sell-out gigs and considerable recording royalties, he felt able to indulge this particular passion. Sadly he was rarely successful and squandered a small fortune.

From an early age he had an eye for the ladies, he found time to enjoy a brief romance with a young Ella Fitzgerald, a fellow member of the Chick Webb Orchestra. But it was his marital arrangements that became particularly entangled. He contrived to marry his second wife Ida before divorcing his first wife Julia thus becoming a bigamist. By the time he was married to wife number three, Fleecie, he was still having regular 'liaisons' with showgirls. As Louis got into bed alongside Fleecie, who was sitting up having just finished paring her feet with a sharp knife, what was said will never be known but then she lunged at him cutting Louis across the right side of his face and stabbed him numerous times in the chest and stomach. When he tried to protect himself with his hands she stabbed them also. She was charged with assault with a deadly weapon, charges he dropped as they reconciled! The good lady exacted an even sweeter revenge when she divorced Louis. Earlier he had used her name as a co-composer of the hit tune 'Caldonia' with Dave Dexter, the original creator. Louis was signed with another publishing company and this subterfuge was designed to conceal his royalties. However, come the divorce Fleecie, lived up to her name, insisting that she indeed was co-composer and therefore entitled to the royalties from Louis' biggest selling record. As he got older he grew bitter as the taxman was chasing him. Undaunted Louis went on to marry wife number four, Martha a calm and resolute lady who stayed with him until his death in 1975.

LOUIS JORDAN'S 'CHOO CHOO CH'BOOGIE'

American music owes a considerable debt to the railroad for its inspiration and, in the tradition of 'Night Train', 'Take The 'A' Train' amongst others, Louis Jordan comes up with this little anthem. In just over two and a half minutes he relates the tale of a guy taking a ride on a train to look for work, but when he reaches his destination and scans the local paper 'the only job vacant needs a man with a knack, so put it right back in the rack, Jack.'

This guy is a train lover 'I just love the rhythm of the clickety-clack', and resolves to live in a beaten up shed down by the railroad: 'So when I hear the whistle, I can peep through the crack, and watch the train a rollin' when it's haulin' the jack.'

Around this simple vignette of daily life, Jordan uses the drummer to emulate the 'clickety clack' while his band echo the sound of the wailing train horn. To top it all, the leader takes a brief, economic but exuberant alto sax solo in the middle to put his instrumental stamp on the proceedings. Confined by the limits of the 78 r.p.m. single, Jordan's recorded solos were never long-winded excursions, but rather a series of concise gems and on this number he blows one of his best.

Jordan possessed the ability to create musical cartoons that captured, by means of a witty, colloquial narrative and rhythmic, punchy playing, incidents of real life in a cameo of three minutes or less. This track (no pun intended) bears convincing testimony to his art.

Chuck Berry: *'If I had to work through eternity, it would be (listening to) Louis Jordan.'*

Louis Jordan On CD

1. The Complete Aladdin Sessions. EMI CDP 796567/2.
2. Best of Louis Jordan. MCA MCAD 4079.
3. Louis Jordan and his Tympany Five. JSP CD 905.

Here's a list of some of Louis' recordings for you to check out: *Ain't Nobody Here But Us Chickens, Saturday Night Fish Fry, GI Jive, Caldonia, Reet Petite And Gone.*

BIG JAY McNEELY
**1927-
Tenor Sax**

'I play to move people, no matter how much I have to give out to do it. I want people to feel the music the way I do. You see, I get a sort of glow when I blow. I think my fans do too.'

Real name: Cecil James McNeely. The President of Savoy records decided Cecil wasn't hip enough and re-christened him 'Big Jay'. The West Coast Hollywood fans called him 'The Go Go Go Man!'

BIG JAY'S SHOWMANSHIP

After the Second World War, the saxophone was used to inject an enormous dose of showmanship into the field of Rhythm and Blues music. In the age of Honkers and Screamers, Big Jay McNeely emerged as an uncontrollable whirlwind. His stage act developed into a wild affair. Tracked by his brother Bob on baritone sax, he would pace the stage, or take off into the auditorium. Then he would strip off his jacket, kneel for the audience and then lie on his back, feet in the air - still blasting away on his horn. Crowds went crazy in response to Big Jay's full-on extrovert showmanship.

Big Jay had received formal training as a jazz musician, and had even blown with Charlie Parker who was a lodger at his house when visiting L.A. 'My mother even washed Charlie Parker's clothes one time!'

By 1947, he felt he was 'losing his soul' so abandoning all the jazz theory, he concentrated his considerable energy and talent on performing with his band around the clubs and dance halls of his hometown, where his exuberant act gained him an enormous following. In 'Downbeat' mag, a feature appeared 'Big Noise in R&B: McNeely, McSqueally - Either Way You Pronounce It, It Means Box Office.'

In 1947, he obtained a recording deal with Savoy, a major jazz label, with whom he cut 'Deacon Hop' which was to become his first hit. He persuaded Ralph Bass, President of Savoy (who had never seen him live) to allow his band to open at the forthcoming jazz concert, headlined by Ben Webster. On the night, Big Jay true to form, drove the jazz audience to near hysteria by lying on his back and honking for 30 minutes solid, until the police, fearing a riot, demanded his removal! Ironically, Webster who, as we know, was no mean honker himself, was so stunned and demoralised, that he at first refused to take the stage, and a shell-shocked Ralph Bass had to resort to threats to enforce his contract!

Webster was in good company. During Big Jay's career, other notable headliners who banned him from their shows included Nat King Cole, crooner Johnny Ray and the mighty Count Basie.

BIG JAY'S ART OF UPSTAGING

Paul Williams, a fellow honker, had enjoyed a national hit with his dance novelty 'The Hucklebuck' and recalled appearing on the same bill.

'We played the first set and then Big Jay went on and played at least an hour. I mean one solo at a time! The drummer took a solo, Big Jay changed his outfit, drank a beer and went backstage, suitably refreshed. The drummer finished his solo, Big Jay took over and played right through until the end of the dance.'

Paul Williams, the headliner, never got back on stage. Big Jay was the forerunner of the extended solo, something Coltrane also adopted, only Big Jay could do it on his back!

In 1950 he opened in L.A.'s Wrigley Field for Lionel Hampton, in front of a 30,000 crowd. After one number Hamp's wife dragged Big Jay off stage because he was stealing the show. When 'Hamp' marched his band down to play, Big Jay ran up into the audience and started to play solo, to the noisy delight of his hometown crowd. 'Hamp' to compete, marched his band around the field so Big Jay crawled on his back across the field and into the dugouts, still playing and another star attraction had been vanquished.

His offstage excursions became infamous. He'd honk outside clubs, and motorists would reply causing traffic chaos. He'd cakewalk to the dressing room in a green suit and emerge later in a purple one, but playing his tenor sax non-stop throughout. When at New York's Band Box he would march around Birdland next door and return with a dozen or so converts in

tow. In San Diego he left his band in the Eagle Ballroom, causing such commotion in the street that he was arrested and had to call his brother from the cells to bail him out. Half an hour later, unabashed he rejoined his band on stage and continued his solo as if there had been no interruption!

To keep ahead of his imitators he stripped his horn and repainted it with gold leaf and fluorescent paint. When the lights went down all that could be seen was Big Jay's horn glowing as he moved around the darkened stage.

Big Jay quit touring soon after he got married in 1960 and then became a Jehovah's Witness. The McNeely Brothers retired from full time playing in the 60s with Big Jay doing the odd gig while working for the Post Office!

He spent the next twenty years being a hardworking religious father, but in 1983 he was persuaded to participate in a revival concert, Battle of the Saxes with former contemporaries and honking rivals Joe Houston and Chuck Higgins. True to form he charged into the auditorium dressed in a black jumpsuit picked out with neon eyeballs. Once on stage his honking became even more crazed as he lay on his back, legs kicking in the air like a fly in its death throes. The youthful audience that had been weaned on the excesses of punk rock, took him to their hearts.

Then in 1984 he was brought over to the U.K. playing the 100 Club for what Black Echoes magazine acknowledges as 'the best little gig in two years or more!' Since the 80s he has toured Western and Eastern Europe, the Far East and Australia spreading the honking gospel according to Big Jay. The legend of Big Jay McNeely refused to lie down - except when blowing some serious sax on stage!

BIG JAY'S 'DEACON HOP'

After a deceptively lazy statement of the theme, he takes off for real. Wailing, bleating, the occasional honk, McNeely drives on remorselessly and then, the handclaps and hi-hats are back for one last statement. His humour is on display as he finishes with a tongue in cheek slur, (if physically possible) while a trumpet toots briefly over the top.

This is a fine example of Big Jay's sound - swaggering, wailing and honking tenor, a rock and roll backbeat and a surging band. Despite his musical pyrotechnics, frenzied gymnastics and over the top showmanship, one has the feeling he never took himself too seriously. This is not to deny his ability, he could show great emotion when the blues demanded it. But like Louis Jordan before him, he could combine consummate musicianship, with dazzling razzmatazz and yet exude an underlying feeling of good humour.

In the awesomely arrogant Little Richard's estimation, Big Jay was 'the only cat who could warm them up for someone like me.'

Big Jay On CD

1. Big Jay in 3-D. King 650.
2. The Big Horn -The History Of The Honkin' and Screaming Saxophone. Proper Box 61.
3. Swingin' - Big Jay McNeely and his band. Collectables 5133.

Here's a list of some recordings by Big Jay for you to check out: *Blow Big Jay, Roadhouse Boogie, There's Something On Your Mind, Tandalayo, Jay's Frantic, Man Eater.*

KING CURTIS
1934-1971
Alto, Tenor and Saxello

Real Name: Curtis Ousley. Nicknamed 'King' because at High School he already ruled as the outstanding tenor sax player.

Aretha Franklin says King Curtis' horn spoke directly to her 'King Curtis was a Soul superhero.'

THE KING OF THE SOUL SAX

His soul saxophone style was the result of taking a singer's approach to a melody. 'I can take a record by a singer, and I can play the identical vocal version on my horn.'

King Curtis probably performed on more record sessions, credited and uncredited, than any other Saxman. His tone varied from the novelty effect that he originated for The Coasters hit, 'Yakety Yak' through the typical R&B blasts found on 'Memphis Soul Stew' to the sensuous lyricism featured on his classic 'Soul Serenade'. It was this versatility that made him such a sought after session musician, but throughout he was identified by his distinctive soul voice.

Although he made his living as a Soul musician either in the studio or touring with the Atlantic Soul Revue, he nevertheless managed to record some outstanding jazz and blues albums as well as performing in jazz clubs around New York.

THE KING'S BRIEF REIGN

Famous Atlantic Records producer Jerry Wexler held him in the highest regard: 'His was a mighty presence. Six foot one, powerful, cool and radiant, he was always in charge. He loved to eat, play sax, shoot crap, ride his cycle and make shrewd deals with music makoffs. He had an endless parade of great players in his bands, including Jimi Hendrix. He was a fine producer and if he was in town when I was recording he was always next to me in the booth, a fountain of terrific ideas and suggestions. No charge.'

Songwriter Mort Schuman: 'He would come in with those mohair suits, you know like you could see him three blocks away on a foggy London night! I mean, it would just shine out there.'

Soul singer Ben E. King: 'At the end of the day's session, everybody would congregate at Curtis' home - at least a dozen people, Aretha Franklin, Cornell Dupree, Eric Gale, most of the session guys, his door was always open. Until he had passed, we didn't realize what a centre we had lost.'

Contrast this with Joseph McNamara, New York Daily News: 'He was a nice guy. But he had a temper and he wouldn't take any nonsense from anybody.'

A child prodigy, while at High School, he was earning 240 dollars a week from his gigging in all the juke joints in Fort Worth, comfortably exceeding the salary of his school principal.

On Sunday afternoons, he always appeared at 'The Paradise Inn' run by a friend, and noted for its 30 foot bar, which during his rendition of 'Night Train' he would get up and 'walk' in the tradition of the great honking tenors.

During his prolific but curtailed career, he estimated that he backed more than 200 artists over 1000 sessions, including Sam Cooke, Bobby Darin, Clyde McPhatter, Laverne Baker,

Brook Benton, Isley Brothers, Connie Francis, and Freddie King.

Eventually he became Musical Director to the Queen of Soul, Aretha Franklin. She claimed she always sang best when the King was by her side, and it was his presence that cajoled her into the studio, when she was experiencing temperamental moods. Their partnership produced a veritable catalogue of soul classics.

Though rarely out of the studio as a session man, in 1962 he emerged into the public spotlight, performing his self-penned 'Soul Twist' which became a Number 1 R&B hit.

King Curtis was to continue his relationship with the Twist rage. Arthur Murray, founder of New York's most prestigious dance school decided to record a twist album which included a dance manual. The result was 'Arthur Murray's Twist Party' in a sleeve complete with instructions illustrated by footprints and dotted lines indicating step sequences. The star of the album was the wonderful hard blowing saxophonist King Curtis, who also provided the vocals. Astonishingly, this has become a cult album amongst his fans and changes hands for ridiculous money.

Due to the endless demand for his services, both in the studio and touring, it would be easy to consider him exclusively a Soul/Rock and Roll artist. This would be a serious oversight. Working, performing and recording with the likes of Freddy King, Champion Jack Dupree and Eddie Kirkland, to name a few, distinguished him as a serious contributor to the Blues scene.

However, his ability as a jazzman, while overshadowed by the sheer volume of his more commercial activities, should not be overlooked. Bassist Chuck Rainey, a long term member of his band, recalled that during matinee performances the King would blow jazz standards. His saxophone peers, including Illinois Jacquet, Ben Webster and Willis Jackson attended expecting to mock the 'jazzman turned rock'n'roller'. Instead they were so overwhelmed by his playing that they deemed it too risky to join him on stage! Further confirmation of his ability as a jazzman can be found on three albums he recorded for Prestige..New Scene of King Curtis and Soul Meeting, both with cornetist Nat Adderley and Wynton Kelly on piano, as well as Soul Battle with fellow saxmen Oliver Nelson and Jimmy Forrest. All three albums were recorded in 1960 - a great year for jazzman King Curtis and jazz fans alike!

He was a perfectionist as a musician in the studio or playing live...and he expected the same standard from all his fellow performers. They soon realised that the wrath of a powerfully built six-footer was best avoided. He applied the same meticulous approach when appearing on stage. At each venue he would produce his toolbox and rewire the sound system to replicate that of the studio where originally recorded. Then, after the gig, he would take time to return the system to it`s original state. Truly a man of many talents!

He was 'shrewd' and multitalented, possessing the ability to draw up a contract, make a deal, put a band together and direct a recording session. Apart from owning property, he also ran his own music publishing business 'that makes more money than I do as a performer. Every musician should find another means of making a living.'

However, he was a notorious gambler, a vice he indulged in the company of the jazz musicians, Brother Jack McDuff, Willis Jackson, and Danny Richmond. Domestically his life did not run smoothly and he left his wife for teenager Modeen

Broughton with whom he lived for seven years until his untimely death.

This occurred at the hand of a junkie on the steps of his apartment block. When he refused to move on, possibly the King's temper took over, and in the ensuing scuffle the vagrant stabbed him to death. Over one thousand mourners attended his funeral at which the Reverend Jesse Jackson, Stevie Wonder and Aretha Franklin contributed their various talents. He was only thirty seven with his finest years to come, but his recorded work remains as a fitting memorial.

An incredibly loyal band of enthusiasts of King Curtis' music evolved in the UK, with worldwide membership, to the extent that a fanzine appeared called 'The Boss'.

KING CURTIS' 'SOUL SERENADE'

Probably the best known track under his own name is 'Memphis Soul Stew' the funky soul dance number where Curtis introduces each instrument in the musical concoction he is cooking up. However, there is one track which epitomises the man's style and genius, and will stand the test of time as a memorial.

'Soul Serenade' was written by Curtis and his is the definitive interpretation. In under 3 minutes it displays so many of his talents. It has a wonderful melodic feel; the gift to express sadness, passion and fire; his clean soaring tone; his ability to swing at all times, whether he's blowing ballads, blues or uptempo ravers.

The song builds from a wistful beginning through an ever increasing intensity until, by the end, Curtis is swinging fiercely and pouring his passion into the horn, culminating in a long held haunting note as it fades into the night. Despite attempts to add lyrics to this beauty, his sax playing has more eloquence and passion than any songwriter could achieve.

In the words of Atlantic Records Producer Jerry Wexler: *'He was noble, ballsy and streetwise like nobody I ever knew. I love him, and even though Down Beat won't give him houseroom, he belongs forever with Pres and Sonny Rollins and Trane.'*

King Curtis on CD
1. King Curtis plays the great Memphis Hits. King Size Soul KOCH KOCD 8015.
2. King Curtis Live at Fillmore.
3. King Curtis: Soul Meeting. Prestige PR CD 24033-2.
4. Best Of King Curtis. Capitol Jazz CDP7243 8 3650422.

Here's a list of some of King's recordings for you to check out: *Whole Lotta Love, Whiter Shade Of Pale, Everything's Gonna Be Alright, For Its Worth, Memphis Soul Stew, I Never Loved A Man, Soul Street.*

JUNIOR WALKER
1940-1995
Alto/Tenor Sax and Vocals

Real Name: Autry De Walt. Nicknamed Walker because as a child he would walk everywhere.

'I didn't worry much when it came time to go, no. Motown helped me gold-plate my horn. But Motown never did teach me how to blow it.'

Painting by Felicity Bowers

THE PARTY STYLE OF JUNIOR WALKER

During the 60s Tamla Motown established itself as a major label and it was certainly one of the most successful and musically influential organisations of the decade. Its records provided some of the most vibrant, exciting and memorable sounds on the scene, and brought Soul music out of the ghetto to the public at large.

But while its sound seemed raw and uninhibited, particularly in comparison to the mass produced white pop music that dominated the charts, founder Berry Gordy and his staff applied the production line philosophy of their own Detroit car makers to achieve a manufactured, polished end product. There was an underlying formula to the musical structure, songs were matched to artists by a form of internal market research, and Gordy himself applied a ruthless standard of quality control.

All the singers were taught deportment, elocution and were tutored in public relations. The female artists were even shown the 'approved' manner of emerging from a car with decorum!

To this sanitised, choreographed and controlled environment, Junior Walker's arrival must have seemed like a return to the swamp. He represented the unrestrained exuberance of a previous, less civilised age. He descended directly from the honoured blood line of the honkers and screamers of the 40s and 50s, the swashbuckling tradition created by the heroes of the chittlin circuit, the likes of Joe Houston, Lynn Hope, Paul

Williams, Hal 'Cornbread' Singer and our own Big Jay McNeely.

Whereas Motown aspired to peak time TV, Hollywood and even Las Vegas, Mr. Walker's domain was the greasy roadhouse on the edge of town, and his music evoked images of low-life characters, illicit deals and short-term liaisons. The courtly matrons who ran the Motown charm school were to encounter their worst nightmare.

'I am a roadrunner. Ever since Berry Gordy told me to scare up a truck and git. I got the truck and lit. I travel. I blow some. People dance. And I like it.'

Walker the showman blew with a raucous, gut-bucket sound, his sax in turn groaning, rasping, bellowing, screeching, squeaking, and straining. He would play standing, from a crouch, or even lying on his back in venues as wide ranging as a Mississipi riverboat to a Ukrainian community hall turned punk palace. Every show a party.

Walker felt a kinship with other Soul saxmen: 'We make a wind to blow them blues clean to Monday. It's Saturday night now, ain't it? And if you'll excuse me, I got a job to do.'

THE LIFE OF A ROADRUNNER

A trio of famous hardblowing Saxmen - Earl Bostic, Illinois Jacquet and Gene Ammons - used to come to Junior Walker's home town, and a youthful and eager Walker, who only started at 18, used to join them.

'We made a lot of noise, people would complain, but the cops would say "hell leave 'em be. At least we know where they are, and they ain't causing no trouble" and they let us play as much as we wanted.'

Colman Andrews comments on Walker's tone reflect the paradox of how Walker despite being subjected to the notorious Motown Charm School still retained his raw, untamed stage presence.

'There is a Detroit saxophone style, which is usually fairly rich and thick, somewhat leisurely, overtly lyrical and sometimes breathy... Walker certainly has some of these elements... and a strong dose of the Texan style... rough, earthy, guttural, but jaunty... he has synthesised into his own saxophone voice a good many of these elements.'

In later years, for commercial reasons, Walker was forced to tone down his raunchy style, resulting in covers of hits by 'The Supremes' and restrained instrumentals like 'A Walk In The Night'. Despite this record producers were never able to completely suppress his unique tone.

He only started singing by accident, when one of the Motown vocalists failed to turn up for his session and Walker was forced into this role out of necessity. Modestly, he dismissed his voice: 'I prefer playing my 'crooked horn' to singing because I can't sing!'

However he was unduly modest, as his vocal manner, is so natural and understated. His version of 'How Sweet It Is To Be Loved By You' while never challenging Marvin Gaye's original, through a combination of Junior's rich, exuberant sax duetting with his own, raw, warm voice, provided another hit version of the song on its own merits.

WALKER'S 'SHOTGUN'

The compulsive track 'Shotgun' was the first hit for Motown having 'the kick of a mule and the greasy feel of a pigs feet dinner'... flying high in the US 100 Billboard pop charts.

It was so called because Walker and his All-Stars were playing a club in 1965 when he noticed a couple of kids dancing doing this different kind of dance, 'doing a two-handed sawing kind of step, looking as though they were cradling a pump-action double barreled shot-gun.'

Hence the name of the track. The track itself was raw and uninhibited and for Motown like nothing it had previously put out. 'Shotgun' broke all the Motown rules of the sleek and winning production format of sweet soul vocalising.

As Bobby Gallagher wrote in the July 1976 edition of Black Music: 'The sound of a gunshot belches out. Before the smoke

has had time to clear, a bullying drum pattern imposes itself only to be quickly distracted by a whining, bleating tenor sax. This is the first 4 seconds of 'Shotgun' a record which leaves you with no choice of description - it has to be termed compulsive. The telling combination of the sledgehammer rhythm, and the helter-skelter horn and the interplay between the shuddering organ and the stark vocal chants, rules out the use of any other adjective.'

This music incorporated the showmanship of Louis Jordan, the unhinged wailing of Big Jay McNeely, and swaggering funk of King Curtis. Junior Walker forged a sound of his own while maintaining the tradition of his illustrious predecessors.

'I am just into makin' a joyful noise. No, I never did take to playin' no real sad songs. I leave that to the other men talkin' through this kind of horn.'

Junior Walker on CD
1. Junior Walker. Anthology. Motown 314530828-2.
2. Junior Walker Home Cookin'. Motown 314530402-2.
3. Shotgun and Soul Session. Motown 017080-2.

Here's a list of some Junior's recordings for you to check out: *Shake And Fingerpop, Tune Up, Come See About Me, How Sweet It Is, I'm A Roadrunner, Walk In The Night.*

CONCLUSION

Well, here we are at the end of our musical journey and what, we hope, has been a voyage of discovery. The purpose of the preceding chapters was to provide an understanding and appreciation of the lives of fourteen outstanding saxophonists as well as an insight into their diverse and frequently intriguing characters. Each in his own way has contributed significantly to the development and evolution of the art of the sax. And of course, all are indebted to Father Sax who set the standard in every way.

At the time of writing, three of our heroes are still with us. Sonny Rollins, now in his 80s, still performs in public and records outstanding albums. Ornette Coleman, another venerable octogenarian, is established as the godfather of avant-garde and, likewise, is still a performer and recording artist. Big Jay McNeely, arguably the 'maddest' of them all, lives quietly with his family, nominally retired, but on occasion has been lured to one-off festival appearances.

Two of the original number, Louis Jordan and Junior Walker, died of natural causes, while the mighty King Curtis was stabbed to death still in his prime.

All of our fourteen were exposed by their working environment to drink and/or drugs. We quoted Dexter Gordon earlier 'it was a little difficult to remain Mr Clean' and while drink was a long established factor - it certainly hastened the demise of

Coleman Hawkins and Ben Webster - drugs, particularly heroin, provided a seriously destructive influence on many lives. The late great jazz vocalist Anita O'Day, compared her first experience of heroin to being 'immersed in a warm bath - totally relaxed and free of daily concerns, protected from the outside world.' Sadly what started as an occasional 'treat' became a daily need and, finally, a full blown addiction. So many great musicians were hooked and it created yet another complication to an already hectic lifestyle. In addition to getting gigs, finding a room, travelling to a new district or town, a prime worry became the urgent need to find a drug dealer at every new location. And in the background to this activity there was the constant threat of arrest and severe periods of incarceration.

Undeniably, heroin influenced the direction of many careers but it was an illness, an addiction not necessarily a madness. However, in the case of Stan Getz, any man who foregoes a night with Ava Gardner to keep a date with his drug peddler, must surely be certifiable!

Putting aside all the pressures that musicians were subjected to, was there a common factor, 'a madness that linked our chosen saxmen?' While there is no readily identifiable physical or mental characteristic, we believe there existed, to varying degrees, one particular element - OBSESSION. To become a great saxophonist 10,000 hours plus needs to be devoted to playing, listening and honing your musical skills. But in addition our heroes possessed an almost selfish single-minded character. John Coltrane epitomised this intense focus by constantly searching for 'the next level', 'wiping the mirror clean' and always moving on. Sonny Rollins no longer frequents the bridges of Manhattan, but is still striving for perfection and practicing for up to 8 hours a day.

So perhaps obsession was the common madness shared by all our saxmen. The overwhelming desire to be the best in their field, while remaining true to their beliefs. In pursuit of these goals, they created some of the finest, most exciting and often most beautiful music ever. Hopefully, our book will inspire you to seek out their amazing legacy of recordings, or even consider the saxophone for yourself. Whatever, we guarantee you will experience hours of pleasure and, like us, have some fun on the journey.

'My life is music. And in some vague, mysterious, and subconscious way, I have always been driven by a taut inner spring which has propelled me to almost compulsively reach for perfection in music, often in fact, mostly at the expense of everything else in my life.' Stan Getz.

BIBLIOGRAPHY

Joachim-Ernst Berendt	*The Jazz Book*, Lawrence Hill Books (7th edition, 2009)
John Broven	*Rhythm & Blues in New Orleans*, Pelican Publishing Co (1998)
Stan Britt	*Long Tall Dexter*, Quartet Books (1989)
John Chilton	*The Song Of The Hawk*, Quartet Books (1990)
Richard Cook; Brian Morton	*Penguin Guide to Jazz*, Penguin (5th edition, 2000)
Bill Crow	*Jazz Anecdotes*, Oxford University Press (2005)
Francis Davis	*Outcats*, Oxford University Press (1990)
Miles Davis; Quincy Troupe	*Miles: The Autobiography*, Picador Books (1990)
Sharon Davis	*Motown: The History*, Guinness Publishing (1988)
Jim Dawson	*Nervous Man Nervous*, Big Nickel Publications (1994)
Wayne Enstice; Paul Rubin	*Jazz Spoken Here*, Da Capo Press (1994)
John Fordham	*The Sound Of Jazz*, Hamlyn (1989)
John Fordham	*Jazz*, Dorling Kindersley (1993)
John Fordham	*Master Blowers*, The Guardian (25 April 1992)
Peter Gammond	*The Decca Book of Jazz*, Frederick Muller (1990)
Nelson George	*Where Did Our Love Go?* Omnibus Press (2003)
Charlie Gillett	*The Sound of the City*, Da Capo Press (2nd edition, 1996)
Ted Gioia	*West Coast Jazz*, University of California Press (1998)
William P. Gottlieb	*Golden Age Of Jazz*, Quartet Books (1979)
Robert Gordon	*Jazz West Coast*, Quartet (1990)
Peter Guralnick	*Sweet Soul Music*, Mojo Books (2002)
Jeff Hannusch	*I Hear You Knockin'*, Swallow Publications (1985)
Milt Hinton; David Berger	*Bass Line*, Temple University Press (1988)
Gerri Hirshey	*Nowhere To Run*, Southbank Publishing (2006)
Wally Horwood	*Adolphe Sax; His Life and Legacy*, Egon Publishers Ltd (1983)
Barry Kernfield (Ed.)	*New Grove Dictionary of Jazz*, Macmillan (1994)
Maurice Lindsay (Ed.)	*The Music Quotation Book*, Robert Hale Ltd (1992)
Martin Lindsay	*Teach Yourself Jazz*, English Universities Press (1958)
John Litweiler	*Freedom Principle: Jazz after 1958*, Blandford Press (1985)
John Litweiler	*Ornette Coleman: the Harmolodic Life*, Quartet Books (1992)
Donald L. Maggin	*Stan Getz: A Life in Jazz*, William Morrow & Co (1996)

Barry McRae	*The Jazz Handbook*, Longman (1987)
Richard Palmer	*Stan Getz*, Apollo Press (1988)
Art & Laurie Pepper	*Straight Life: the Story of Art Pepper*, Canongate Books (2001)
Lewis Porter	*Lester Young*, University of Michigan Press (2nd edition, 2006)
David H Rosenthal	*Hard Bop*, Oxford Paperbacks (1994)
Ross Russell	*Bird Lives!* Da Capo Press (1996)
Nat Shapiro; Nat Hentoff	*Hear me Talkin' To Ya*, Souvenir Press Ltd (1992)
Bill Shoemaker	*Cleaning the Mirror*, Downbeat Magazine (July 1992)
Ben Sidran	*Talking Jazz: an Oral History*, Da Capo Press (1995)
Chip Stern	*Rollins: the Cross and the Rose*, Musician magazine (May 1988)
Jerry Wexler	*Rhythm and the Blues*, Jonathan Cape Ltd (1994)
Valerie Wilmer	*As Serious as your Life*, Serpent's Tail (1999)

Honkers and Screamers - booklet by Joop Visser, accompanying 'The Big Horn' CD - 'The History of Honkin' & Screamin' Saxophone, Proper Records, 2003

David Was Q Mag - article by David Was in Q Magazine, August 1992, p.40

Other BLOWOUT SAX BOOKS are available:

1. BLOWOUT SAX - A REVOLUTIONARY APPROACH. THE BEGINNERS SAX BOOK.
2. BLOWOUT LATE AND SPIRITUAL SAX. AS/TS
3. BLOWOUT THE GREATEST POP SAX. AS/TS
4. BLOWOUT SOLO SAX. AS/TS
5. BLOWOUT HONKERS SWINGERS AND SCREAMING SAX. AS/TS
6. BLOWOUT SUPERGROOVY 60'S SAX BABY YEAH. AS/TS

7. BLOWOUT THE KING OF SOULSAX. AS/TS
8. BLOWOUT BLUE SAX PART 1. AS/TS
9. BLOWOUT BLUE SAX PART 2. AS/TS
10. BLOWOUT THE KINGS OF JAMAICAN SAX. AS/TS
11. BLOWOUT THE SAXPERIMENTALISTS. AS/TS
12. BLOWOUT SMOOTH OPERATORS. AS
13. BLOWOUT SAX TENOR TITANS. TS
14. BLOWOUT THE PURE THE BEAUTIFUL AND THE POET OF SAX SOUNDS. AS/TS
15. BLOWOUT THE SOULSAX BROTHERS. AS/TS
16. BLOWOUT THE PINK PANTHER SAX SOUND. TS
17. BLOWOUT SAX EPICS. AS
18. BLOWOUT THE GRANDPAPPYS OF BOOGALOO AND SOUL MAKOSSA SAX. AS
19. BLOWOUT FAT FUNK SAX. AS/TS. Over 450 transposed tunes. Ready as a syllabus and for the saxophone market as playalongs and jamalongs.
20. BLOWOUT SAX MADMEN.
21. BLOWOUT SAXOLOGY.
22. THE GUIDE TO RUNNING A SUCCESSFUL BLOWOUT SAX SCHOOL.

Please visit **www.blowoutsax.com** for more details.